NORTHROP FRYE is University Professor of English at the University of Toronto.

This volume is a reprint of a work originally published in 1965. The first four essays deal with *Paradise Lost*, and are based on the Centennial Lecture Series which marked the one-hundredth anniversary of Huron College, University of Western Ontario. The fifth discusses the structure and content of *Paradise Regained*.

"For those who know the work of Professor Northrop Frye ... this will be a further example of his unobtrusive learning, his wit, and his singular power of critical systematisation." *British Book News*

THE RETURN OF EDEN

Five Essays on Milton's Epics

NORTHROP FRYE

UNIVERSITY OF TORONTO PRESS
Toronto and Buffalo

© University of Toronto Press 1965
Toronto and Buffalo
Reprinted in paperback 1975
Printed in USA
ISBN 0-8020-1654-3 (cloth)
ISBN 0-8020-6281-4 (paper)
LC 65-6968

TO A. B. B. MOORE

Preface

THE FIRST FOUR CHAPTERS OF THIS BOOK were originally the
Centennial Lectures delivered at Huron College in March,
1963, under the title "A Tetrachordon for *Paradise Lost*." This
title was somewhat spoiled by the addition of a revised version
of an earlier paper of mine, "The Typology of *Paradise
Regained*," which appeared in *Modern Philology* in May, 1956.
I am indebted to Principal Morden and Professor Blissett of
Huron College for many kindnesses, and to the University of
Chicago Press for allowing me to reprint the substance of my
article from *Modern Philology*.

The lectures at Huron College were conceived as an introduction to *Paradise Lost* for relatively inexperienced students,
with the hope that they would also have something to interest
the general reader. They have grown more complicated as I
have rewritten them for publication, but this is still their main
intention. Perhaps if I say that they are a distillation of under-
graduate lecture notes their function will be more clearly
understood. As is inevitable when one writes more than once
on the same subject, there is some repetition with other writings
of mine. The first chapter expands several points summarized
in my introduction to an edition of Milton which was published
in 1950 and is still in print, and the second chapter explains
once more the framework of Renaissance imagery which is

already explained in my *Fables of Identity* and elsewhere. However, the advantage of this repetition is that the present book is a complete argument in its own right.

N.F.

Victoria College in the
University of Toronto
September, 1964

Contents

THE RETURN OF EDEN

The Story of
All Things

I SUPPOSE ANYONE PROPOSING TO DELIVER a series of lectures on *Paradise Lost* ought to begin with some explanation of why he is not deterred from doing so by the number of his predecessors. If my predecessors had all failed, I could at least claim the merit of courage, like the youngest adventurer of so many folk tales who is also the brashest and most bumptious of the whole series. But many of them have succeeded better than I expect to do, and I have no knowledge of Milton sufficiently detailed to add to the body of Milton scholarship or sufficiently profound to alter its general shape. I am talking about Milton because I enjoy talking about Milton, and while I may have begun the subject of these lectures late, it was not long in choosing. Huron College is a hundred years old, and though I find, on checking the dates, that I have not been teaching Milton for quite that long, I have been teaching him long enough to have incorporated him as a central part of my own literary experience. Consequently I feel that I can approach Milton with some sense of proportion based on the fact that his proportions are gigantic. Every student of Milton has been rewarded according to his efforts and his ability: the only ones who have abjectly failed with him are those who have tried to cut him down to size—their size—and that mistake at least I will not make.

The second edition of *Paradise Lost* opened with two complimentary poems addressed to Milton, one in English by Andrew Marvell and one in Latin by Samuel Barrow. The Barrow poem begins with a rhetorical question. When you read this wonderful poem, he says, what do you read but the story of all things? For the story of all things from their first beginnings to their ultimate ends are contained within this book:

> Qui legis Amissam Paradisum, grandia magni
> Carmina Miltoni, quid nisi cuncta legis?
> Res cunctas, et cunctarum primordia rerum,
> Et fata, et fines continet iste liber.

Implicit in what Barrow says is a standard Renaissance critical theory. It will be familiar to most readers, but I need it again because its elements reappear as structural principles in *Paradise Lost*. It was generally assumed that in literature there were inherently major genres and minor genres. Minor poets should stick to the minor genres, and should confine themselves to pastorals or to love lyrics. Minor genres were for poets of minor talents, or for professional poets learning their trade, or for poets too high in social rank to be much interested in publication or in any kind of poetic utterance beyond the kind of graceful conventional verse that is really a form of private correspondence. The major poets were those for whom the major genres were reserved; and of these, the most important in Renaissance theory were epic and tragedy.

The epic, as Renaissance critics understood it, is a narrative poem of heroic action, but a special kind of narrative. It also has an encyclopaedic quality in it, distilling the essence of all the religious, philosophical, political, even scientific learning of its time, and, if completely successful, the definitive poem for its age. The epic in this sense is not a poem by a poet, but that poet's poem: he can never complete a second epic unless he is the equal of Homer, and hence the moment at which the epic poet chooses his subject is the crisis of his life. To decide to write an epic of this kind is an act of considerable courage, because if one fails, one fails on a colossal scale, and the echo of ridicule may last for centuries. One thinks of what the name "Blackmore" still suggests to students of English literature, many of whom have not read a line of Blackmore's epics. Further, the epic can only be completed late in life, because of the amount of sheer scholarship it is compelled to carry. In Gabriel Harvey's phrase, major poets should be "curious universal scholars," but it takes time to mature a scholar and still more time to unite scholarship with poetic skill. Of course this theory implies that Homer was a poet of encyclopaedic learning, but it was almost a critical commonplace to assume that he was: William Webbe, for example, speaks of "Homer, who as it were in one sum comprehended all knowledge, wisdom, learning and policy that was incident to the capacity of man."

The epic, as a poem both narrative and encyclopaedic, is to be distinguished from the long poem which is simply one or the other. A narrative poet, as such, is a story-teller, and a story-teller is in the position of a modern novelist: the more stories he tells the more successful he is. One thinks of Ariosto's *Orlando Furioso* and of the question addressed to the author by the Cardinal who was supposed to be his patron: "Where did you find all these silly stories, Messer Lodovico?" This remark, however inadequate as criticism, does indicate something of the quality of the romance genre that Ariosto was using, for the romance tends to become an endless poem, going on from one story to another until the author runs out of stories to tell. The encyclopaedic poem, again, was a favourite genre of the Renaissance. The two poets of this group whom we should now rank highest, Lucretius and Dante, were somewhat disapproved of in Protestant England on ideological grounds, and a more tangible influence on Milton was *La Sepmaine* of du Bartas, which displayed so much knowledge of the creation that its author was compelled to expand the divine activity into two weeks. Some other encyclopaedic poems, such as Palingenius' *Zodiac of Life*, which, as translated by Barnabe Googe, may have been one of Shakespeare's school books, were based on rather facile organizing schemes—in other words their scholarship was a matter of content rather than of poetic structure. Romances, particularly *The Faerie Queene*, could also achieve an encyclopaedic quality by virtue of being allegorical, when they not only told stories but when their stories meant things in moral philosophy and political history—"Where more is meant than meets the ear," as Milton says.

But although there were many encyclopaedic poems and many romances and narratives, and although the authors of both genres were highly respected, still the central form with the greatest prestige was the epic. And the ideal, the huge, impossible ideal, would be a poem that derived its structure from the epic tradition of Homer and Virgil and still had the quality of universal knowledge which belonged to the encyclopaedic poem and included the extra dimension of reality that was afforded by Christianity. Now, says Samuel Barrow, who would ever have thought that anyone could actually bring off such a poem? But it's been done, and by an English poet too:

> Haec qui speraret quis crederet esse futurum?
> Et tamen haec hodie terra Britanna legit.

For in the seventeenth century, writing such a poem in English was still a patriotic act, with a certain amount of conscious virtue about it, as writing poetry on this side of the American border has now. The first critical statement ever made about *Paradise Lost*, therefore, tells us that *Paradise Lost* is among other things a technical *tour de force* of miraculous proportions.

That Milton was fully aware of the size and scope of what he was attempting, and that he shared the assumptions of his age about the importance of the epic, hardly need much demonstrating. For him, of course, the responsibilities entailed by the possession of major poetic talent were only incidentally literary: they were primarily religious. The word "talent" itself is a metaphor from a parable of Jesus that seems to associate the religious and the creative aspects of life, a parable that was never long out of Milton's mind. The analogy between the Christian and the creative life extends even further. A Christian has to work hard at living a Christian life, yet the essential act of that life is the surrender of the will; a poet must work hard at his craft, yet his greatest achievements are not his, but inspired.

Milton's first major poem, the one we know as the Nativity Ode, ends its prelude with the self-addressed exhortation:

> And join thy voice unto the angel choir
> From out his secret altar touched with hallowed fire.

In a sense this is the key signature, so to speak, of Milton's poetry: his ambition as a poet is to join the tradition of inspired prophetic speech that began with the great commission to Isaiah. When he speaks in *Paradise Lost* of wanting to justify the ways of God to men, he does not mean that he wishes to do God a favour by rationalizing one of God's favourite parables: he means that *Paradise Lost* is a sacrificial offering to God which, if it is accepted, will derive its merit from that acceptance. The Nativity Ode is closely related to the Sixth Elegy, addressed to Diodati, where Milton distinguishes the relaxed life permitted the minor poet who writes of love and pleasure from the austerity and rigorous discipline imposed by major powers. One is a secular and the other a priestly or dedicated life. The reason for the discipline is not so much moral as spiritually hygienic. To be a fit vessel of inspiration the poet must be as genuinely pure as the augur or pagan priest was ceremonially pure:

> Qualis veste nitens sacra, et lustralibus undis
> Surgis ad infensos augur iture Deos.

After the first period of Milton's poetry had reached its climax with the two great funeral elegies, *Lycidas* and *Epitaphium Damonis*, Milton started making plans for poetry in the major genres—perhaps part of the meaning of the "fresh woods and pastures new" at the end of *Lycidas*. His *Reason of Church Government*, in a famous passage, mentions in particular three genres, the tragedy, the "diffuse" or full-length epic, and the "brief" epic. This last is still a somewhat undeveloped conception in criticism, though examples of it in English literature stretch from *Beowulf* to *The Waste Land*. One cannot help noticing the similarity between this list of three major genres and the *Samson Agonistes*, *Paradise Lost* and *Paradise Regained* produced so many years later. At that time, Milton tells us, he was thinking of Arthur as the subject for his "diffuse" epic. But of course he had still many years to wait before he could give his full attention to writing it. The simultaneous pull in Milton's life between the impulse to get at his poem and finish it and the impulse to leave it until it ripened sufficiently to come by itself must have accounted for an emotional tension in Milton of a kind that we can hardly imagine. That the tension was there seems certain from the way in which the temptation to premature action remains so central a theme in his poetry. The tension reached a crisis with his blindness, yet his blindness, as he had perhaps begun to realize by the time he wrote *Defensio Secunda,* eventually gave him, as deafness did Beethoven, an almost preternatural concentration, and was what finally enabled him to write of heaven, hell and the unfallen world on his own terms.

In the same passage of *The Reason of Church Government* Milton speaks of doing something for his own nation of the same kind as Homer and Virgil, "with this over and above, of being a Christian." This additional advantage means for him partly a technical poetic advantage as well. For what gave the encyclopaedic poem such prestige in Christian civilization was the encyclopaedic shape of Christian philosophy and theology, a shape derived ultimately from the shape of the Bible. The

Bible, considered in its literary aspect, is a definitive encyclopaedic poem starting with the beginning of time at the creation,
ending with the end of time at the Last Judgment, and survey-
ing the entire history of man, under the symbolic names of
Adam and Israel, in between. Explicitly Christian poetry had
moved within this framework from earliest times. Bede's
Ecclesiastical History, one of the authorities used by Milton for
his history of Britain, tells how English poetry began with the
poet Caedmon, who was ordered by an angel to sing him
something. Being inspired by a Christian muse, Caedmon
began promptly with a paraphrase of the first verses of Genesis
on the creation, worked his way down through the Exodus
and the main episodes of the Old Testament to the Incarnation,
and went on to the Last Judgment and the life eternal. The
dramatic cycles of the Middle Ages are another example of the
effect of the shape of the Bible on English literature.

The sermon, in Milton's day, constituted a kind of oral epic
tradition dealing with the same encyclopaedic myth. The
proverbially long Puritan sermons, divided into anything from
eighteen to twenty-five divisions, usually owed their length to
a survey of the divine plan of salvation as it unrolled itself from
the earliest prelapsarian decrees to the eventual consummation
of all things. This oral tradition has been embedded in *Paradise
Lost* in the four hundred lines of the third book which constitute
a sermon of this type preached by God himself. The speech of
Michael, which takes up most of the last two books of *Paradise
Lost*, is a summary of the Bible from the murder of Abel to the
vision of John in Patmos in which the biblical myth takes the
form of a miniature epic or epyllion, and as such pulls together

and restates all the major themes of the poem, like a stretto in a fugue.

Renaissance critics believed that there were major and minor genres for prose as well as for poetry, as they made much less of the technical distinction between prose and verse than we do. In prose the major genres were mainly those established by Plato: the Socratic dialogue form, and the description of the ideal commonwealth. Such works as Sidney's *Arcadia* were highly praised because they were felt to belong to this tradition, as we can see in the discussion of the *Arcadia* in the opening chapter of Fulke Greville's biography of Sidney. But the Renaissance was above all a great age of educational theory, and its educational theory, to which Milton contributed, was based squarely on the two central facts of Renaissance society, the prince and the courtier or magistrate. Hence the educational treatise, which normally took the form of the ideal education of prince, courtier or magistrate, had even greater prestige in Renaissance eyes than the description of the ideal commonwealth.

The Classical pattern for the treatise on the ideal education of the prince had been established by Xenophon in the *Cyropaedia*, which Sidney describes as "an absolute heroical poem," thus implying that it represents the prose counterpart of the encyclopaedic epic. Spenser, in the letter to Raleigh which introduces *The Faerie Queene*, makes it clear that this encyclopaedic prose form is also a part of the conception of his poem, and speaks of his preference for Xenophon's form to Plato's, for a practicable as compared to an impossible ideal. Milton also shows a touch of impatience with Plato and with what he calls Plato's "airy burgomasters," and we should expect him to be of Spenser's mind in this matter. And just as the encyclopaedic shape of the Bible is condensed into the speech of Michael, so the speech of Raphael versifies a major prose genre, for the colloquy of Raphael and Adam is a Socratic dialogue without irony, a symposium with unfermented wine, a description of an ideal commonwealth ending with the expulsion of undesirables, and (for Adam is the king of men) a cyropaedia, or manual of royal discipline. It is essentially the education of Adam, and it covers a vast amount of knowledge, both natural and revealed.

The tradition of the epic was, of course, established by Homer in the *Iliad* and the *Odyssey*, but these two epics represent different structural principles. Many Classical scholars have noted that the *Iliad* is closer in form to Greek tragedy than it is to the *Odyssey*. The *Odyssey*, the more typically epic pattern, is the one followed more closely by Virgil in the *Aeneid* and by Milton in *Paradise Lost*. Of the characteristics which the *Odyssey*, the *Aeneid* and *Paradise Lost* have in common, three are of particular importance.

In the first place, there are, in the form in which we have them, twelve books, or a multiple of twelve. Milton published the first edition of *Paradise Lost* in ten books to demonstrate his contempt for tradition, and the second edition in twelve to illustrate the actual proportions of the poem. He had been preceded in his conversion to a duodecimal system by Tasso, who had expanded the twenty cantos of *Gerusalemme Liberata* into the twenty-four of *Gerusalemme Conquistata*. Spenser, too, is preoccupied with twelves: each book has twelve cantos and the total number of books planned was either twelve or twenty-four. We shall try to suggest in a moment that the association of Milton's epic with this sacred and zodiacal number may be less arbitrary than it looks.

Secondly, the action of both the *Odyssey* and the *Aeneid* splits neatly in two. The first twelve books of the *Odyssey* deal with the wanderings of the hero, with the journey through wonderlands of marvels and terrors, the immemorial quest theme. The next twelve books never leave Ithaca (except for the katabasis at the end, in a part of the poem often considered a later addition), and their action is that of a typical comedy of recognition and intrigue, as the unknown and ridiculed beggar eventually turns out to be the returning hero. The first six books of the *Aeneid* have a similar quest pattern; the next six, the account of the struggle of Aeneas with the Italian warlords, also has the structure of romantic comedy, full of compacts, ordeals and other traditional features of comic action, and ending in success, marriage, and the birth of a new society. In both epics the main interest shifts half way from the hero's private perils to his social context. In the letter to Raleigh, Spenser, with a reference to Tasso, also distinguishes private or princely from public or kingly virtues in the epic theme. This division of narrative between a quest theme and a theme of the settling of a social order has a biblical parallel in the story of the Exodus, where forty years of Israel's wandering in the wilderness are followed by the conquest and settlement of the Promised Land. Milton preserves the traditional feature of a split in the middle of the action when, at the beginning of Book Seven, he says that the action for the second half of the poem will be confined to the earth. The order in *Paradise Lost* is the reverse of the biblical one, as it starts with the Promised

Land and ends in the wilderness; but the biblical order is preserved when we add *Paradise Regained* to the sequence.

But of course of all the traditional epic features, the most important is that of beginning the action *in medias res*, in Horace's phrase, at a dramatically well-advanced point and then working back simultaneously to the beginning and forward to the end. If we ask beginning and end of what, the answer is, beginning and end of the total action, of which only a part may be presented in the actual poem. This total action is cyclical in shape: it almost has to be because of the nature of the quest theme. The hero goes out to do something, does it, and returns. In the *Odyssey*, the total action begins when Odysseus leaves Ithaca and goes off to the Trojan War, and it ends when he gets back to Ithaca as master of his house again. Matters are less simple in the *Iliad*, but even there the total movement of the Greeks out to Troy and back home again is clearly in the background. In the *Aeneid* there is what from Milton's point of view is a most important advance in this conception of a total cyclical action. Here the total action begins and ends, not at precisely the same point, but at the same point renewed and transformed by the heroic action itself. That is, the total action of the *Aeneid* begins when Aeneas leaves Troy collapsing in flames, losing his wife; and it ends with the new Troy established at Rome, Aeneas remarried and the household gods of the defeated Troy set up once again in a new home. The end is the beginning as recreated by the heroism of Aeneas.

We notice that the trick of beginning the action at a dramatically well-advanced point is not done entirely at random. The *Odyssey* begins with Odysseus at the furthest point from home, on the island of Calypso, subjected to the temptations of Penelope's only formidable rival. The action of the *Aeneid* similarly begins with Aeneas' shipwreck on the shores of Carthage, the *Erbfeind* or hereditary enemy of Rome and the site of the citadel of Juno, Aeneas' implacable enemy. Similarly, the action of *Paradise Lost* begins at the furthest possible point from the presence of God, in hell. The cycle which forms the total background action of *Paradise Lost* is again the cycle of the Bible. It begins where God begins, in an eternal presence, and it ends where God ends, in an eternal presence. The foreground action begins *in medias res,* translated by Milton in his Argument as "in the midst of things," with Satan already fallen into hell, and it works from there back to the beginning and forward to the end of the total action. The foreground action deals with the conspiracy of Satan and the fall of Adam and Eve, and the two speeches of the two angels deal with the rest of the cycle. Raphael begins with what is chronologically the first event in the poem, the showing of Christ to the angels, and brings the action down to the point at which the poem begins. After Adam's fall, Michael picks up the story and summarizes the biblical narrative through to the Last Judgment, which brings us back again to the point at which God is all in all. The epic narrative thus consists of a foreground action with two great flanking speeches where the action is reported by messengers (*aggeloi*) putting it in its proper context.

We notice that in the Classical epics there are two kinds of revelation. There is the kind that comes from the gods above, when Athene or Venus appears to the hero at a crucial point with words of comfort or advice. There is nothing mysterious about these appearances: they happen in broad daylight and their function is to illuminate the present situation. Athene appears in the disguise of Mentor to give Telemachus the kind of advice that a wise and kindly human being would also give. There is another kind of revelation which is sought from gods below. Telemachus gains it by disguising himself as a seal and catching Proteus; Odysseus gains it by a complicated and sinister ritual of sacrifice, the spilling of blood, ghosts and darkness. There are strong hints that knowledge obtained in this way is normally forbidden knowledge, and it does not illuminate a present situation: it is specifically knowledge about the future. It is knowledge about his own future that Odysseus seeks when he calls up Teiresias from hell; it is knowledge of the future of Rome that Aeneas gets when he descends, though with less ritual elaboration, into the cave guarded by the Sibyl. The association of future and forbidden knowledge is carried even further in Dante's *Inferno*, because the people in Dante's hell have knowledge of the future but not of the present.

The kind of knowledge given to Adam in Michael's speech is essentially a knowledge of the future, of what is going to happen. It is intended to be consoling, although Adam collapses twice under the ordeal of being consoled, and the fact that knowledge of the future is possible means of course that the freedom of human will has been mortally injured. The suggestion is clearly that such knowledge of the future is a part of the forbidden knowledge which Adam should never have had in the first place, knowledge which God is willing to give him but which Satan would have cheated him out of. Human life now is in large part a dialectic between revelation and the knowledge of good and evil, and this dialectic is represented in *Paradise Lost* by the contrast between God the Father and Adam after his fall. God the Father sits in heaven and foreknows what will happen, but, as he carefully explains, not forcing it to happen. Below him is Adam in a parody of that situation, foreknowing what is going to happen to the human race in consequence of his fall, but unable in the smallest degree to interfere with or alter the course of events.

The foreground action, the conspiracy of Satan and its consequences, forms a kind of mock-Telemachia in counter-point to the main epic action to be considered in a moment, a parable of a prodigal son who does not return. Technically, however, the foreground action presents a sharp focusing of attention which brings it close to dramatic forms. The fall itself is conceived in the form of tragedy, the great rival of epic in Renaissance theory, yet almost the antithesis of the epic, as it demanded a concentrated unity of action which seems the opposite of the epic's encyclopaedic range. The ninth book represents a crystallization of Milton's earlier plans for treating the fall of man in tragic form, with Satan as a returning spirit of vengeance persuading Eve into a foreshortened compliance much as Iago does Othello. Nature, sighing through all her works, occupies the place of the chorus.

At the opening of the poem we find ourselves plunged into the darkness of hell and eventually, after our pupils have expanded, look around and see one or two lights glaring. We then realize that these are eyes, and a number of huge clouded forms begin to come out of a kind of sea and gather on a kind of shore. Throughout the first two books we move through shadowy and indefinite gloom, and then, at the opening of the third, are plunged quite as suddenly into blinding light, where only after our pupils have contracted again can we observe such details as the pavement of heaven which "Impurpled with celestial roses smiled." We feel that such intensities are appropriate to a poet who is not only blind but baroque, and who, if he never saw the shadows of Rembrandt or the sunlight of Claude, still reflects his age's interest in chiaroscuro. But the principle *ut pictura poesis* can only be expressed in verbal spectacle, and we should also realize the extent to which the dramatic form of the Jonsonian masque has informed these first three books, a dark and sinister antimasque being followed by a splendid vision of ordered glory. The masque vision moves slowly from heaven down through the starry spheres to Eden; the antimasque modulates into the ludicrous disorder of the Limbo of Vanities, and disappears until it is recalled by Raphael's narrative of an earlier expulsion from heaven.

There is, then, with the dramatic foreground action and the speeches of Raphael and Michael filling in the beginning and end of the total background action, a kind of formal symmetry of a type that we might not expect in a poem that we have just called baroque. I think that this formal symmetry can be carried much further, and I should like to divide the total action in a way which I think best illustrates it. Some of the divisions take up several books and others only a few lines, but that is of no importance. Most of the shorter ones are from the Bible, and Milton expected his reader to be able to give them their due importance. Let us visualize the dial of a clock, with the presence of God where the figure 12 is. The first four figures of the dial represent the four main events of the speech of Raphael. First comes the first epiphany or manifestation of Christ, when God the Father shows his Son to the angels and demands that they worship him. This is the chronological beginning of the total action, as already remarked. Next, at 2 on the dial, comes the second epiphany of Christ at the end of the war in heaven, when on the third day he tramples on the rebel angels and manifests himself in triumph and wrath. The third stage is the creation of the natural order, as described by Milton in his extraordinarily skilful paraphrase of the Genesis account. The fourth phase is the creation of the human order, with the forming of the bodies of Adam and Eve, in the account of which Adam takes over from Raphael.

After this the foreground action moves across the lower part of the dial. At the figure 5 comes the conspiracy of Satan, ending in his pact with Sin and Death. The generation of Death from Satan is a parody of the generation of the Son from the Father which starts off the action, Death being, so to speak, the Word of Satan. At 6, the nadir of the action, comes the tragic catastrophe, the fall of Adam and Eve, the fall, that is, of the human order established by God. Next, at 7, comes the fall of the natural order, which is really a part of the fall of Adam and Eve, and is described in Book Ten as the triumph of Sin and Death, corresponding to Satan's pact with them at 5.

The next four stages are the ones covered by the speech of Michael: they correspond to the four that we found in the speech of Raphael, but are in roughly the reverse order. First, at 8, comes the re-establishing of the natural order at the time of the flood, when it is promised with the symbol of the rainbow that seedtime and harvest will not fail until the end of the world. Next, at 9, comes the re-establishing of the human order, when the law is given to Israel and the prototype of Jesus, Joshua, who has the same name as Jesus, takes possession of the Promised Land. Next, at 10, comes the third epiphany of Christ, the Incarnation properly speaking, which again is an epiphany ending with the triumph over death and hell in a three-day battle. Next, at 11, comes the fourth epiphany of Christ, the Last Judgment, again an epiphany of triumph and wrath, when the final separation is made between the orders of heaven and of hell. At 12, we come back again to the point prophesied by God himself in his speech in Book Three, when he says that there will come a time when he will lay by his sceptre and "God shall be all in all." The final point in the vast cycle is the same point as the beginning, yet not the same point, because, as in the *Aeneid*, the ending is the starting point renewed and transformed by the heroic quest of Christ. Thus there can be only one cycle, not an endless series of them. To summarize:

1. First epiphany of Christ: generation of Son from Father.
2. Second epiphany of Christ: triumph after three-day conflict.
3. Establishment of the natural order in the creation.
4. Establishment of the human order: creation of Adam and Eve.
5. Epiphany of Satan, generating Sin and Death.
6. Fall of the human order.
7. Fall of the natural order: triumph of Sin and Death.
8. Re-establishment of the natural order at the end of the flood.
9. Re-establishment of the human order with the giving of the law.

10. Third epiphany of Christ: the Word as gospel.
11. Fourth epiphany of Christ: the apocalypse or Last Judgment.

There are four orders of existence in *Paradise Lost*, the divine order, the angelic order, the human order and the demonic order. Being an epic, *Paradise Lost* has to deal with the traditional theme of the epic, which is the theme of heroic action. In order to understand what heroic action was to Milton we have to think what a Christian poet would mean by the conception of heroic action: that is, we have to ask ourselves what for Milton a hero was, and, even more important, what an act was. Milton says clearly in *The Christian Doctrine* what he means by an act. An act is the expression of the energy of a free and conscious being. Consequently all acts are good. There is no such thing, strictly speaking, as an evil act; evil or sin implies deficiency, and implies also the loss or lack of the power to act. There is a somewhat unexpected corollary of this: if all acts are good, then God is the source of all real action. At the same time, as Milton says, or rather as his sentence structure says in spite of him, it is almost impossible to avoid speaking of evil acts:

It is called actual sin, not that sin is properly an action, for in reality it implies defect; but because it commonly consists in some act. For every act is in itself good; it is only its irregularity, or deviation from the line of right, which properly speaking is evil.

What happens when Adam eats the forbidden fruit, then, is not an act, but the surrendering of the power to act. Man is free to lose his freedom, and there, obviously, his freedom stops.

His position is like that of a man on the edge of a precipice—
if he jumps it appears to be an act, but it is really the giving up
of the possibility of action, the surrendering of himself to the
law of gravitation which will take charge of him for the brief
remainder of his life. In this surrendering of the power to act
lies the key to Milton's conception of the behaviour of Adam.
A typically fallen human act is something where the word
"act" has to be in quotation marks. It is a pseudo-act, the
pseudo-act of disobedience, and it is really a refusal to act at all.

Implied in this argument is a curious paradox between the
dramatic and the conceptual aspects of the temptation scenes
in Milton's poetry. In a temptation somebody is being persuaded to do something that looks like an act, but which is
really the loss of the power to act. Consequently, the abstaining
from this kind of pseudo-activity is often the sign that one
possesses a genuine power of action. The Lady in *Comus,* for
example, has a somewhat uninteresting dramatic role: she is,
in fact, paralysed, and, dramatically, says little except an
eloquent and closely reasoned paraphrase of "no." Comus
attracts a good deal more of our sympathy because his arguments are specious, and therefore dramatically more interesting.
Yet we have to realize that the real situation is the opposite of
the dramatic one. It is Comus who represents passion, which is
the opposite of action; it is the Lady who holds to the source
of all freedom of action. The same situation is even more
sharply manifested in the role of Jesus in *Paradise Regained,*
where Jesus behaves, for four books, like a householder dealing
with an importunate salesman. Yet again what is actually
going on is the opposite of what appears to be going on. Satan,
who seems so lively and resourceful, is the power that moves

toward the cessation of all activity, a kind of personal entropy that transforms all energy into a heat-death.

The typical demonic "act" is not a real act either, but it is a much more concentrated parody of divine action. It has the quality not of disobedience but of rebellion, and it differs from the human act in that it involves rivalry, or attempted rivalry, with God. The appearance of Nimrod at the beginning of the last book of *Paradise Lost* represents the coming into human life of the demonic, of the ability to worship devils, of turning to Satan for one's conception of the kingdom and the power and the glory, instead of to God. What Satan himself manifests in *Paradise Lost* is this perverted quality of parody-heroism, of which the essential quality is destructiveness. Consequently it is to Satan and his followers that Milton assigns the conventional and Classical type of heroism. Satan, like Achilles, retires sulkily in heaven when a decision appears to be favouring another Son of God, and emerges in a torrent of wrath to wreak vengeance. Like Odysseus, he steers his way with great cunning between the Scylla-like Sin and the Charybdis-like Death; like the knights errant of romance, he goes out alone on a perilous quest to an unknown world. The remark the devils make about the war in heaven, that they have sustained the war for a day "And, if one day, why not eternal days?" opens up a perverted vision of eternity as a Valhalla of endless strife.

It is only the divine that can really act, by Milton's own definition of an act, and the quality of the divine act reveals itself in *Paradise Lost* as an act of creation, which becomes an act of re-creation or redemption after the fall of man. Christ, therefore, who creates the world and then recreates or redeems man, is the hero of *Paradise Lost* simply because, as the agent or acting principle of the Father, he is ultimately the only actor in the poem.

The angelic order is there to provide models for human action. They have superior intellectual and physical powers which man may eventually attain, but in *Paradise Lost* they are moral models only. They form a community of service and obedience, often doing things meaningless to them except that as the will of God they have meaning. They are ministers of responsibility (Gabriel), instruction (Raphael), command (Michael) or vigilance (Uriel). The figure of the tense, waiting angels, listening for the Word to speak and motionless until it does, appears in the last line of the Nativity Ode and again in the last line of the sonnet on the poet's blindness. Such angels are, as the angel says to John at the end of the Bible, fellow servants of mankind: there is nothing in Milton of Rilke's "schrecklich" angel.

More important than any of these, for the theme of heroism, is Abdiel, who remains faithful to God in the midst of the revolted angels. Abdiel, like many people of unimpeachable integrity, is not a very attractive character, but everything he says in the poem is of the highest importance. The speech which he makes to Satan at the time of the war in heaven indicates that he is establishing the pattern of genuine heroism that is later to be exhibited in the life of Christ, the "better part of fortitude" which consists primarily in obedience and endurance and in the kind of courage that is willing to suffer under ridicule and contempt and a chorus of opposition. As Abdiel says to Satan, after being restored to the faithful angels, "My sect thou seest." This pattern is followed in the biblical visions which Michael shows to Adam: in the story of Enoch, the one just man who stands out against all the vice of his time, and receives the angelic reward of direct transportation to heaven, and in Noah, who is similarly the one just man of his time and is saved from an otherwise total destruction. It could have been exemplified by Lot in Sodom, which is referred to briefly by Milton. This is the pattern which is followed by the prophets and apostles, and nobody else is entitled to be called heroic.

Doubtless the faithful angels could have defeated the rebels by themselves, but the symbolism of the three-day war in heaven is designed to show that the total angelic power of action is contained in the Son of God. The angels have no strength that does not come from God, and the devils have no strength against God at all. It is difficult not to feel that the entire war in heaven is a huge practical joke to the Father, all the more of one because of the seriousness with which the devils take it. The admiring description of the size of Satan's spear and shield in Book One has two perspectives: from man's point of view Satan is incalculably strong, but from God's point of view he is only a lubber fiend. God's own conception of strength is represented by the infant Christ of the Nativity Ode, the genuine form of Hercules strangling the serpent in his cradle, physically weak and yet strong enough to overcome the world.

In this world spiritual strength, being a direct gift of God, is not necessarily accompanied by physical strength, though it is normally accompanied by physical invulnerability. This condition is the condition of chastity, traditionally a magical strength in romance, and the theme of the magic of chastity runs all through Milton. The Lady cannot be hurt by Comus because of the "hidden strength" of her chastity. Samson owes his physical strength to his chastity, to his observance of his Nazarite vow: as he says bitterly, God hung his strength in his hair. He loses his chastity when he tells Delilah what his secret is. Such chastity does not in his case imply virginity or even continence: two marriages to Philistine women do not affect it, nor apparently does even a visit to a Philistine harlot, which Milton ignores, though he read about it in the Book of Judges. Adam and Eve have been given more than mortal strength by their chastity, which is also not affected by sexual intercourse: they lose their chastity only by eating of the forbidden tree. A reference to Samson in Book Nine establishes the link in the symbolism of chastity between the two.

Like most morally coherent writers, Milton is careful to distinguish the human from the demonic, even when what he is showing is the relation between them. As it may be difficult to feel this distinction without examples we may take an analogy from Shakespeare. Cleopatra in Shakespeare is all the things that the critics of Milton say Eve is. She is vain and frivolous and light-minded and capricious and extravagant and irresponsible and a very bad influence on Antony, who ought to be out chasing Parthians instead of wasting his time with her. She is morally a most deplorable character, yet there is something about her which is obstinately likable. Perhaps that makes her more dangerous, but it's no good: we cannot feel that Cleopatra is evil in the way that Goneril and Regan are evil. For one thing, Cleopatra can always be unpredictable, and as long as she can be that she is human. Goneril and Regan are much closer to what is meant in religion by lost souls, and what that means dramatically is that they can no longer be unpredictable. Everything they do or say is coarse and ugly and cruel, but still it also has about it something of the stylized grandeur of the demonic, something of the quality that Milton's devils have and that his human beings do not have. At the same time Cleopatra is a part of something far more sinister than herself: this comes out in the imagery attached to Egypt, if not in the characterization attached to her. Putting the two together, what we see is the human contained by the demonic, a fascinating creature of infinite variety who is still, from another point of view, sprung from the equivocal generation of the Nile.

It is the same with Adam and Eve. Theologically and conceptually, they have committed every sin in the calendar. In *The Christian Doctrine* Milton sets it all down: there was nothing bad that they omitted to do when they ate that wretched apple:

It comprehended at once distrust in the divine veracity, and a proportionate credulity in the assurances of Satan; unbelief; ingratitude; disobedience; gluttony; in the man excessive uxoriousness, in the woman a want of proper regard for her husband, in both an insensibility to the welfare of their offspring, and that offspring the whole human race; parricide, theft, invasion of the rights of others, sacrilege, deceit, presumption in aspiring to divine attributes, fraud in the means employed to attain the object, pride, and arrogance.

Yet this is something that it is wholly impossible for us to feel or realize dramatically, nor does Milton attempt to make us do so. Eve may have been a silly girl but she is still our general mother, still quite obviously the same kind of human being that we are. What has happened is that human life is now attached to the demonic, this being one of the points made by Michael, especially in the vision of Nimrod, the archetypal tyrant, the tyrant being one of the clearest examples of a human being who has given himself up to the demonic.

The fact that conventional heroism, as we have it in Classical epic and medieval and Renaissance romance, is associated with the demonic in Milton means, of course, that *Paradise Lost* is a profoundly anti-romantic and anti-heroic poem. Most of us live our lives on a roughly human level, but if we meet with some setback, snub, imposed authority or other humiliation we are thrown back on something that will support and console us, and unless we are saints that something is likely to be the ego. The sombre, brooding, humourless ego, with its "high disdain from sense of injured merit" drives us to look for compensation, perhaps by identifying ourselves with some irresistible hero. If in this state we read Milton, we shall find his Satan, so far from being the author of evil, a congenial and sympathetic figure. If we later regain a better sense of proportion, we may understand something of the profundity and accuracy of Milton's conception of evil.

Satan is a rebel, and into Satan Milton has put all the horror and distress with which he contemplated the egocentric revolutionaries of his time, who stumbled from one party to another and finally ended precisely where they had started, in a cyclical movement with no renewal. There is an almost uncanny anticipation of some of the moods of later Romanticism, also an age of egocentric revolutionaries. In particular, there is a quality in Milton's treatment of the demonic world that can only be called Wagnerian: in the unvarying nobility of the rhetoric, in the nihilistic heroic action that begins and ends in the lake of fire, in the *Götterdämmerung* motif in the music of hell:

> Others, more mild,
> Retreated in a silent valley, sing
> With notes angelical to many a harp
> Their own heroic deeds, and hapless fall
> By doom of battle, and complain that Fate
> Free virtue should enthrall to force or chance.

This is not to say that Wagner is a demonic artist, any more than that Milton is a Satanist, only that there are demonic elements portrayed in Wagner that some very evil people have found, as many have found Satan, irresistibly attractive.

The anti-heroic tendency in Milton is, however, less complicated than his attitude to myth, of which it forms part. When a literary critic says that the story of the fall of man is a myth, he is not making any statement about the truth of its content, merely that it is a certain kind of story; but still his feeling about its truth is coloured by this very shift of attention from its content to its form. But Milton is never tired of stressing the difference in ethical content between the truth of the Bible and the fables of the heathen, and obviously the story of the fall would never have interested him if he had not believed it to be as literally true as the events of his own life. The story of *Paradise Lost* is a myth in the sense that the action or narrative movement (*mythos*) is provided by a divine being: the essential content is human, and as credible and plausible as Milton's source would allow him to make it. The marvels and grotesqueries of the poem, such as the building of Pandemonium or the Limbo of Vanities, are mostly demonic, and form a contrast to the central action. In modern literature a writer may use a mythical subject because it affords him an interesting and traditional story pattern, as Cocteau does in *Orphée* or Giraudoux in *Antigone*. In Tolstoy's *Resurrection* we have a purely realistic narrative which assumes a shape with the religious significance indicated in the title. Milton's attitude to myth in *Paradise Lost* is much closer, temperamentally and technically, to Tolstoy than it is to Cocteau or Giraudoux.

Myths differ from folk tales or legends in having a superior kind of importance attached to them, and this in turn makes them stick together and form mythologies. A fully developed mythology thus tends, as the Bible does, to take an encyclo-paedic shape. Ovid's *Metamorphoses*, for example, starts with creation and flood stories and works its way down to Julius Caesar as the Bible does to Jesus. Milton's exhaustive use of Ovid is often sympathetic, but evidently he finds in the Ovidian theme of metamorphosis, the identifying of a human figure with an object in nature, the point at which polytheism becomes obvious idolatry. The demonic action of *Paradise Lost* ends with an Ovidian metamorphosis in which the devils are changed to serpents. Satan has taken the form of the serpent; he finds in hell that he cannot get rid of it, but is still a serpent; the devils in looking at him become serpents too:

> what they saw
> They felt themselves now changing.

There is a clear recall of the remark about idols in the 115th Psalm: "they that make them are like unto them."

For us, the mythological imagination is really part of the poetic imagination: the instinct to identify a human figure with a natural object, which gives mythology its sun gods and tree gods and ocean gods, is the same instinct that is described by Whitman:

There was a child went forth every day,
And the first object he look'd upon, that object he became,
And that object became part of him for the day or a certain part
   of the day,
Or for many years or stretching cycles of years.

The author of *Lycidas* would have understood this very well; but a question not relevant to Whitman is relevant to Milton: is this identifying consciousness centred in the ego, as Satan's intelligence is, or not? To identify one's consciousness directly with the works of God in our present world, for Milton, is to enter the forest of Comus on Comus' own terms, to unite ourselves to a sub-moral, sub-conscious, sub-human existence which is life to the body but death to the soul. The free intelligence must detach itself from this world and unite itself to the totality of freedom and intelligence which is God in man, shift its centre of gravity from the self to the presence of God in the self. Then it will find the identity with nature it appeared to reject: it will participate in the Creator's view of a world he made and found good. This is the relation of Adam and Eve to Eden before their fall. From Milton's point of view, the polytheistic imagination can never free itself from the labyrinths of fantasy and irony, with their fitful glimpses of inseparable good and evil. What Milton means by revelation is a consolidated, coherent, encyclopaedic view of human life which defines, among other things, the function of poetry. Every act of the free intelligence, including the poetic intelligence, is an attempt to return to Eden, a world in the human form of a garden, where we may wander as we please but cannot lose our way.

The Breaking of the Music

IN LOOKING AT THE TOTAL CYCLE of events in *Paradise Lost*, we saw that the first event chronologically is the manifestation of Christ to the angels by the Father, the event described by Raphael near the middle of Book Five. There are several difficult points in this scene, and we have to walk warily. In the first place, it looks as though the Father were exhibiting his youngest upstart favourite to a better-established community who had at least the right of seniority; and in regard to Satan, as though some senile whim were making a younger Jacob supplant an Esau who had as yet done nothing to forfeit his birthright. This view of the Son of God as the latest favourite is the superficial view, and consequently it is the one that the devils take, all superficial readers of Milton being in the position of minor devils. But the superficial view is, as usual, the wrong one.

In *The Christian Doctrine*, Milton distinguishes the literal generation of the Son by the Father from the "metaphorical" generation. Where God is concerned, Milton is much more at ease with the literal than with the metaphorical, but there is a real distinction here, the nature of which is explained by Abdiel to Satan later on. Abdiel says that the Son of God is the Word of God, that is, the active agent of God, and as the agent of God, he created all things, including the angels. This may be the Son of God's first epiphany, or manifestation as an objective fact or personality, to the angels, but what the angels are really looking at, including those who are later to revolt, is their own creative principle. By refusing to understand that he is their own creative principle, by resenting or mocking his exhibition, the rebel angels are committing the sin which later reappears in human history as the sin of Ham, the sin that brought so heavy a curse of servitude on Ham and his descendants.

It also appears that the epiphanized Son of God is to the angels something of what the forbidden tree is to man, a provoking object, as Milton calls it in *Areopagitica*, set in front of the angels, hung deliberately in front of their noses as a test of their obedience and as an incident in their own spiritual education. One gets the impression that in some mysterious way there is a drama going on in heaven which corresponds to the drama going on on earth, and that the angels are being educated in the same kind of epic quest that the human race is being educated in. Perhaps this is part of what Raphael means when he says to Adam that earth may be only the shadow of heaven, and that things on earth are much more like things in heaven than is generally believed by Adam's descendants. God the Father says to the angels, quoting from what is eventually going to be the second Psalm:

> This day have I begot whom I declare
> Mine only Son

and to Adam, "in the day that ye eat thereof ye shall surely die." In both oracles there is a mental reservation in the word "day" which angels and Adam alike are required to understand. "This day" to the angels does not mean literal begetting at that moment: "the day" to Adam does not mean literal death at that moment.

In any case, the rebel angels assume that the Son of God is a creature, because they feel that they are also sons of God. But as the Son is the manifest power of God, and as they do not recognize him as such, they are forced to go on to reject the creative power of God itself. In the *Ecclesiastical Polity*, Hooker, in attempting to deal with the question of why some angels revolted in the very presence of God, says that it could only have happened as the result of some sort of "reflex of their understanding upon themselves." In Milton, the rebel angels go through a similar kind of reflex, which takes the form of a curious abstracting quality in their minds. Three aspects of this abstraction are of particular importance in understanding the poem.

In the first place, they abstract the will of God into fatalism. The Son is the will or agent of God, carrying out the divine decrees in the Father's mind: when they reject him, the conception of omnipotent will becomes separated from God, and from the sense of reason and purpose and consciousness which his presence should inspire. This separation obliterates the distinction between Creator and creature: the real creative power, Satan feels, has made him as much of a god as God, and where two gods conflict, there can be no supreme power but fate. Fate is not chance, to be presently considered, and which is the deity of chaos rather than hell. Chance is mindless and automatic: fate is a mysterious and sinister omnipotence to which a demonic being would feel himself impersonally linked, as the Son is personally linked to the Father.

Secondly, as just implied, the rebel angels abstract the personal creative power of God into an impersonal creative power, whose affiliations are with the physical and material. Their invention of gunpowder is a by-product of the demonic instinct to turn for help from the creative power of God to the "originals of nature." Third, and most important, they abstract the two aspects of God's creative power, energy and form, into the categories which we know as time and space. Thus in the later demonic theology, time and space are the official creative forces of the world. Space, says Satan in the council of devils, may produce new worlds. And in reply to Abdiel he says:

> We know no time when we were not as now;
> Know none before us, self-begot, self-raised
> By our own quickening power when fatal course
> Had circled his full orb, the birth mature
> Of this our native Heaven, ethereal sons.

Raphael has already explained to Adam, when he gets to this point in his narrative, that the showing of the Son to the angels took place on a New Year's Day in the great year marked by the precession of the equinoxes, and which takes up twenty-six thousand of our years. It is obvious, therefore, that there are different levels of experiencing and comprehending time and space. In the mind of God time is always a pure present, and past, present and future are all the same point. The ambiguity in the word "day" requires men and angels to sharpen their habitual conceptions of time to understand something of the divine view, which proceeds from a mind where a day and a thousand years are the same. With the angels, time is essentially the variety and rhythm of experience, or, as Raphael explains to Adam:

> We also have our evening and our morn,
> We ours for change delectable, not need.

The experience of time by Adam is similar, but after his fall, human beings began to experience time in the way that we still do, as a combination of a straight line and a circle. The straight line, where there is no real present and everything is annihilated in the past as we are drawn into an unknown future, is the fallen conception of time. The unfailing cycle of seedtime and harvest, established after the flood, represents the element of promise and hope in time, and imitates in its shape the circling of the spheres. To the devils below mankind, time is pure clock time, or simply one moment after another, the kind of experience dramatized by Macbeth in his "Tomorrow" speech.

Similarly with the understanding of space. To God, just as all time is an eternal present, so all space is an eternal presence. For the angels, and for man in Paradise, space has that coherence of form which we attach to the word "home" in our ordinary language. To Adam after the fall, space has become an indifferent environment, and in the demonic conception of space, it has become a world of total alienation. Two famous remarks of Satan indicate this: one is "Which way I fly is hell; myself am hell," the other is

> The mind is its own place, and in itself
> Can make a heaven of hell, a hell of heaven.

The two statements represent very different moods, but are intellectually identical: they both assume a totally objective universe with nothing qualitatively different from it except the egocentric subject.

In refusing to recognize the Son as their own creative principle, then, the devils are closing the gate of their own origin. This theme of closing the gate of origin recurs all through the epic, and is the basis of the feeling which later appears in humanity as what Milton calls shame. Shame to Milton is something deeper and more sinister in human emotion than simply the instinctive desire to cover the genital organs. It is rather a state of mind which is the state of the fall itself: it might be described as the emotional response to the state of pride. It is the state later dramatized in Blake's very Miltonic lyric, "Earth's Answer," in the *Songs of Experience*:

> Does the sower
> Sow by night
> Or the plowman in darkness plow?

In Homer's *Odyssey* Odysseus is placed asleep in a mysterious place called the Cave of the Nymphs, which is said to have two entrances, one used by the gods and the other by mortal men. The conception is similar to Homer's other conception of the two gates of dreams in the *Iliad*, the horn gate of true dreams and the ivory gate of delusory ones. The Cave of the Nymphs

became an important archetype with the Neoplatonic philosopher Porphyry's commentary *De antro nympharum*, and it finds
its way into the symbolism of, at least, Blake and Yeats.
Milton's Paradise also has two entrances, one employed by
God and the angels in descending what was later visualized
as Jacob's ladder, and the other used by Adam when he is
driven out of Paradise down to the "subjected plain." From
then on, and during the whole of human history, the gate of
origin for the entire human race is shut behind us.

In contrast, the gate of heaven opens easily, as though
operated by some kind of electric eye. When Raphael comes
down to instruct Adam, we are told that

> at the gate
> Of Heaven arrived, the gate self-opened wide
> On golden hinges turning.

Similarly when the Son of God comes down to create the
world in Book Seven:

> Heaven opened wide
> Her ever-during gates, harmonious sound
> On golden hinges moving.

But while the gate of heaven opens easily, it shuts easily too,
if the grace its opening symbolizes is not taken advantage of.
Milton says in *The Reason of Church Government*: "The door
of grace turns upon smooth hinges, wide opening to send out,
but soon shutting to recall the precious offers of mercy to a
nation." Man does not evolve toward grace in his own time,
but must seize the eternal moment of heaven when it appears
to him. The gate separating hell from chaos, by contrast, opens

with great and creaking difficulty, but once open, it can never be shut until the Last Judgment, when it becomes the seal on a tomb from which there is no resurrection:

> Both Sin and Death, and yawning Grave, at last
> Through Chaos hurled, obstruct the mouth of Hell
> For ever, and seal up his ravenous jaws.

The conceptions of time and space, then, which are really the energy and form of God's creative power, exist on different levels, depending on the intelligence of the conceiving mind. This is a cosmological fact, and the fall, first of the rebel angels and then of man, elaborates a cosmology. Everybody who has ever had to comment on *Paradise Lost* has had to devote some time to its cosmology, often with some reluctance at having to incorporate what seems the lumber of defunct science in with the living poetry. It would however be better to think of the cosmology of *Paradise Lost* as a framework for the poem's imagery: in that way it does not become merely obsolete science but a part of the structure of the poem itself.

Traditionally, for both medieval and Renaissance poets, and in fact for most poets down to Newton's time, there are four levels of existence, corresponding, with some modifications, to the four orders of existence described in the previous chapter. There is, in the first place, the order of grace or heaven, in the sense of the place of the presence of God. Below this is the proper human order, the way in which God intended man to live, the order represented by the story of the Garden of Eden in the Bible and by the legend of the Golden Age in the Classics. This order, though, in the Psalmist's phrase, "a little lower than the angels," is not, at least in Milton, qualitatively different from the angelic order. Below this again is the physical order into which man is now born, the order to which animals and plants are much better adjusted than he is. Below the physical world is the world of sin and death and corruption, a level which is not really part of nature, in the sense that it was never intended to be there, although of course it permeates the physical world and causes everything alive in it to die. We notice that Christianity has adopted the world-wide primitive belief that there is no such thing as natural death, and that all death is ultimately the result of a personal and malignant agency.

Since the fall, man is born into the third of these four levels of existence, the physical world of animals and plants. He does not belong in it, but is faced from birth with a moral dialectic, and must either rise above it into his proper human home or sink below it into the state of sin, a degradation that the animal cannot reach. Education, religion, law and the habit of virtue are the means by which man may raise himself from the physical order into which he is born to his proper human home where he belongs. That proper home is all that he can now recover of the Paradise in which he was originally placed. If we keep this in mind we shall readily understand Milton's conception of the aim of education as being "to repair the ruin of our first parents by regaining to know God aright." It follows that there are two levels of nature, a physical one and a human one. The forest inhabited by Comus is the physical world in which the Lady is lost and imprisoned: Comus urges her to enter into communion with nature as lived in that world, and his proposal is exactly that of Satan to Eve: "Be wise, and taste." Included in the proposal is the suggestion that such things as sexual promiscuity are innocent, because "natural." The Lady knows that *her* nature is of a different order, and that the argument from Comus' kind of nature is founded on a bad pun.

In Milton's earlier poems, including *Comus*, the starry spheres in the physical world above the earth represent all that is left of nature as God originally planned it. The heavenly bodies are made out of quintessence, which is immortal; they move in perfect circles, the only form proper to their dignity, and they are not subject to sin or decay or mutability. There is a traditional association of the angels with the heavenly bodies: a group of angels called intelligences had them under their particular jurisdiction. We see a vestige of this in *Paradise Lost* when Milton calls Uriel the Regent of the Sun. But there are certain modifications that Milton makes in the traditional picture of the universe. In the first place, heaven itself is a creation of God like the angels, and consequently heaven is a part of the order of nature. The angels in Milton are quite familiar with the conception of nature: Abdiel says to Satan, for example: "God and Nature bid the same." Then again, in *Paradise Lost*, the whole of the order of nature falls with the fall of Adam, and with the fall of nature, as described in Book Ten, the stars turn into beings of noxious efficacy, meeting "in Synod unbenign." *As far as man is concerned* (I italicize this because it is a hinge of Milton's argument), the entire order of nature is now a fallen order. The washing away of the Garden of Eden in the flood symbolizes the fact that the two levels of nature cannot both exist in space, but must succeed one another in time, and that the upper level of human nature can be lived in only as an inner state of mind, not as an outward environment.

In Book Eight Adam asks Raphael, or is obviously preparing to ask him, whether other parts of the starry heavens are inhabited by conscious beings, and is "doubtfully answered."

We are not yet ready to explain why Milton gives so much prominence to the fact that he, and consequently Raphael, cannot answer the question, but it is clear already that the question is unanswerable, within the framework of *Paradise Lost*. To answer a question is to consolidate the mental level on which it is asked, because we can only answer a question by accepting the assumptions in the question. If we ask: "Where is God?" the correct answer is no answer, because the assumption in the question is wrong: the conception of space does not apply to God in this direct way. Adam is asking a question about nature, and the nature of nature, so to speak, depends on Adam's behaviour.

This is the kind of semantic problem that we meet in Milton's discussion of the creation. The opening statement of the Bible is that God made the heavens (i.e., the sky or firmament) and the earth. The reader may naturally ask: "What did he make it out of?" The account goes on to say that God imposed form and light on something described as waste, void, dark, watery and deep. In Milton this something is chaos, and there is an answer to the reader's question: God made the world "out of" matter, in its chaotic state. But if the reader asks further: "Who made matter?" the question is semantically illegitimate. Matter is not "made"; it is not a creation at all. If we push this "What did he make it out of" question beyond its semantic limits, we have to say either "out of nothing," which is really saying that there is no answer, or "out of something coeternal with God," which for Milton is nonsense, though it is the entering wedge of Satan's conception of an independent creative power in nature. We should be better advised to go back to the biblical statement that God made the world and start again. To make something, whether a poem out of the babble of words in our mind or a statue out of a block or marble, is to extend our presence and consciousness into an area where it has not previously been. So with God. Chaos is that into which God's presence chooses not to extend itself; creation is that into which his presence has extended itself.

The traditional diagrams of creation are those of the chain of being and of the Ptolemaic cosmos, and Milton uses what he wants from both. The chain of being is a hierarchy of existence founded on the conceptions of form and matter, the creation and that out of which the creation is made. It stretches from God, who is form without matter, down through the angels to man, who, being half spiritual and half material, is in the exact centre, the microcosmos or epitome of the whole chain, and from there through animals and plants to the mineral world, which is the limit of creation, and from there to chaos, which is as near as we can get to matter without form. In Milton everything created, that is, anything once touched by the presence of God, has implanted in it a tendency to rise upward toward its maker and seek identity with him. For mankind this is an evolution toward a purely spiritual nature. If Adam had not fallen, the evolution would have been physical in process, until, as Raphael explains, "Your bodies may at last all turn to spirit." Now it is primarily a moral process, like that symbolized by the chastity of the Lady in *Comus*:

> Till oft converse with heavenly habitants
> Begin to cast a beam on th' outward shape,
> The unpolluted temple of the mind,
> And turns it by degrees to the soul's essence,
> Till all be made immortal.

The Ptolemaic universe is the environment of the chain of being. God's environment is the upper Heaven or the Empyrean; the lower heaven or sky, which stretches from the *primum mobile* to the moon, is part of the order of nature but not—as yet—a part of man's home. It has the traditional associations with angels we have mentioned, and is the symbolic human home of regenerate man in Dante's *Paradiso*. Below the moon are the spheres of the four elements, fire, air, water and earth. In *Paradise Lost* there appears to be no elemental sphere of fire: we may assume that the traditional sphere of fire is identified with those of the heavenly bodies and the angels guarding them. In the *Vacation Exercise* poem, written early but published later than the first edition of *Paradise Lost*, we gather that the spheres of the elements at one time played a larger role in Milton's imagination:

> Then passing through the spheres of watchful fire,
> And misty regions of wide air next under,
> And hills of snow and lofts of piled thunder,
> May tell at length how green-eyed Neptune raves,
> In Heaven's defiance mustering all his waves.

This passage introduces another important element in Milton's cosmology: the three regions of air. Above the lower air that we breathe is the middle air, a region of intense cold, from which storms and tempests emerge, and from which Death, in one of Milton's earliest poems, descends to carry off an infant dying of a cough. This deathly region could not have existed before the fall: it marks the limit of Satan's conquest of the order of nature and his present headquarters in human life. This is why Paul speaks of him as prince of the power of the air, why witches and other devotees of evil have the power of raising tempests, and why the heathen associated their gods with such places as the top of Mount Olympus, from whence they "ruled the middle air." Above this was the region of upper air, a temperate domain of perpetual spring, the traditional locale of the earthly Paradise. This is where the Garden of Eden is in Dante, where the Gardens of Adonis are in Spenser, and where the Attendant Spirit in *Comus* has his home, a home also associated with the Gardens of Adonis. Eden in *Paradise Lost*, though thought of as on a mountain "above all hills," does not need to be so high up physically. But now that the freezing sphere of middle air has come into human life, that is where it is symbolically. An early sketch of *Paradise Lost* was to have begun with Moses explaining how this upper region has disappeared from human view since the fall.

The four elements are the four possible combinations of the four principles, hot, cold, moist and dry, which in chaos keep forming chance combinations, for chance combinations are at the bottom of Milton's world just as they are at the bottom of the quantum-theory cosmologies of today. Chaos is an ambiguous world, and its moral quality is no exception. Matter, Milton explicitly says, is intrinsically good: there is nothing to be said for the Manichean view that the material is the evil. Evil must come from a perversion of intelligence, and though a corruption of nature, it cannot be an original part of nature. But of course chaos has no power to resist evil, and, not being part of the creation, it exhibits a curious affinity with the evil which conquers it, an affinity symbolized by Satan's pact with Chaos. The fall of the natural order which succeeds the fall of Adam is essentially an entrance of chaos into creation. And just as there is at least an analogy between God's creation and the human power of making things, so there is at least an analogy between chaos and the superstitions produced by ignorance and fantasy. In trying to grasp the shadows of the chaotic world we can never tell where personification stops and abstract nouns begin:

> Orcus and Ades, and the dreaded name
> Of Demogorgon; Rumor next and Chance,
> And Tumult and Confusion all embroiled,
> And Discord with a thousand various mouths.

The poetic effect of such description is: "This is chaos; you can make what you like of it." Milton says that nothing once created can be annihilated, but anything formed by chance in chaos is annihilated by the next chance.

The will of God executes the decrees in the mind of God, and all creatures apprehend that mind in their own way. The angels are carefully educated by God himself in the ways of God: he explains the meaning of events to them, even allows them to eavesdrop on what sound like arguments with himself. The faculty addressed by God in man, both before and after the fall, is the reason, a faculty not essentially different from what the angels have, but slower in the speed of its apprehension: discursive rather than intuitive, as Milton says. Below reason is the instinct which appears in the migratory birds who are "intelligent of seasons." The order of physical nature is a "self-balanced" mechanism, and its emblem is the emblem of justice and equality, the balancing scales which appear at the end of Book Four to indicate, in the appropriate context, that God permits Satan's journey to Eden. I say appropriate context, because the same fact could only be expressed in chaos by chance or accident. We are told that at one point in chaos Satan goes into what would now be called "free fall," and that he would have been falling yet if unluckily he had not happened to strike a solid cloud and bounce back up. There is still more in this deliberately grotesque image, as we shall see in a moment.

The activity of God, of which the central form is creation, is regularly symbolized in Milton by music, though music in Milton has its larger Platonic meaning which includes poetry. We may think of creation as the restraining of chaos by order: this aspect of creation is represented by the musical metaphor of "harmony," in the sense of a stable relationship of parts to a whole. There is "harmony" in heaven, symbolized by the songs of the angels, and when Christ moves into chaos and creates order the angelic music accompanies the act. Creation itself takes the form of spheres, harmoniously moving with a music that Adam could hear before his fall, and the connection between the harmony of the spheres and that of the songs and dances of angels is indicated by Raphael when he speaks of:

> Mystical dance, which yonder starry sphere
> Of planets and of fixed in all her wheels
> Resembles nearest.

In the Nativity Ode also the song of the angels and the music of the spheres are in counterpoint to one another, and at the Incarnation this music is heard for an instant in the fallen world. The chaste soul, like the Lady in *Comus*, achieves a harmony which is attuned to these harmonies of the cosmos, and the elder brother's "divine philosophy" is largely concerned with the attempt to set forth the order, at once musical,

poetic and mathematical, which can "keep unsteady Nature to
her law," in the words of *Arcades*. Poetry and music, the
"Sphere-born harmonious sisters, Voice and Verse," impose
an order on experience which helps us to make this act of
understanding. In the earlier poems particularly, Milton seldom
refers to music without associating it with the original creative
power of the Word of God, a power that still works, partly
through the musical arts, to recreate harmony in the soul of
man. As he says in his epigram on the singer Leonora, some
divine mind teaches harmony to man through her singing, and
her song is the speaking word of that divinity:

> Aut Deus, aut vacui certe mens tertia coeli
> Per tua secreto guttura serpit agens;
> Serpit agens, facilisque docet mortalia corda
> Sensim immortali assuescere posse sono.
> Quod si cuncta quidem Deus est, per cunctaque fusus,
> In te una loquitur, caetera mutus habet.

Such a symbolism would most readily be focused on the
figure of Orpheus, who haunts so many of Milton's early
poems. The art of Orpheus recreated the sympathy between
man and nature which existed in Eden, hence Orpheus represents everything that a human being can do to redeem a soul
from death. Eurydice was only "half regained," but we have
the wistful hope that a poet who had been taught a greater
song than Orpheus knew, singing "With other notes than to
th' Orphean lyre," might succeed better with human souls, if
not with animals and trees. The art of Orpheus suggests magic,
and magic suggests the control of elemental spirits:

> those Demons that are found
> In fire, air, flood, or underground,
> Whose power hath a true consent
> With planet or with element.

Whatever one thinks of magic, a soul as pure as the Lady in
Comus might be able to commune with a harmony in the
sublunary world as well as with the spherical one. The Lady's
virtue is protected by an attendant spirit, also a musician,
descending from the upper air, and by Sabrina, a water-spirit.
In fact all the characters in *Comus* are elemental spirits except
the Lady and her brothers. Comus and his followers are not
what they claim to be, but what they do claim to be is precisely
similar: elemental spirits whose power has a true consent with
the planets:

> We that are of purer fire
> Imitate the starry choir,
> Who, in their nightly watchful spheres,
> Lead in swift round the months and years.

Such a conception of "harmony" is more philosophical than
genuinely musical: it is harmony in the sense of stable and
unchanging relationships, which in terms of music is "perfect
diapason," an everlasting sounding of something like a C major
chord. Music itself may disclose "harmony" as a total form,
but in listening to it we are listening to intricate and energetic
movement:

> Untwisting all the chains that tie
> The hidden soul of harmony.

This suggests that we ought to revise our conception of creation: it is not so much imposing form on chaos as incorporating
energy in form. It would be wrong to overlook Milton's sense
of the "enormous bliss" of nature, the rushing and joyous
power that he had celebrated as early as his Fifth Elegy on the
coming of spring. The frenzied Bacchantes may have been
inspired by the wrong god, but at least they were responding
to the energy that the true God brought out of nature by

creating it, and this kind of enthusiasm, in the conclusion of
Epitaphium Damonis, finds its place in heaven, again in counter-
point to the more decorous songs of Zion:

> Cantus ubi, choreisque furit lyra mista beatis,
> Festa Sionaeo bacchantur et orgia thyrso.

The lion in Book Seven, pawing to get his hinder parts free,
is an eloquent emblem of creation as the emancipating of
energy by form, the same power that reappears in human life
as liberty, the ability to act which is possible only in a state of
internal discipline.

There is demonic music, of course. The song of Comus,
imitating the starry choir, is a demonic parody of the Lady's
Echo Song, which symbolizes a much more genuine kinship
with nature; the "rout that made the hideous roar" in *Lycidas*
is a parody of Orpheus' own songs; the devils in Book One
moving "In perfect phalanx to the Dorian mood" parody the
faithful angels moving

> In silence their bright legions to the sound
> Of instrumental harmony, that breathed
> Heroic ardor to adventurous deeds.

But the general rhythm of the world that God created is clear
enough. The Creator moves downward to his creatures, in a
power symbolized by music and poetry and called in the Bible
the Word, releasing energy by creating form. The creature
moves upward toward its Creator by obeying the inner law
of its own being, its *telos* or chief end which is always and at all
levels the glorifying of God.

It follows that there must be an upward and a downward
demonic movement. The upward one is simple enough: the

destructive explosion from below associated in Milton's mind from earliest days with the Gunpowder Plot. We have already noted that the discovery of gunpowder on the part of the rebel angels was not an accident, but the result of turning from their divine original to the originals of nature. When Satan's foot slips in chaos he is saved by falling on a substance of this nature: "instinct with fire and nitre." In the background is the myth of Antaeus, the giant son of Earth who was strengthened by his mother whenever he fell back on her: the strategic place of this myth in *Paradise Regained* will meet us later. The Limbo of Vanities, the explosion of deluded souls trying to take heaven by storm, repeats the same movement. One of Milton's epigrams on the Gunpowder Plot establishes the link in imagery, and explains why the account of the Limbo of Vanities in *Paradise Lost* suddenly turns into an anti-Catholic tirade. He says that if those in the unreformed church were to throw their cowls and local gods into the sky instead of gunpowder they would have a better chance of reaching heaven:

> Sic potius foedos in caelum pelle cucullos,
>   Et quot habet brutos Roma profana Deos.
> Namque hac aut alia nisi quemque adjuveris arte,
>   Crede mihi caeli vix bene scandet iter.

The downward demonic movement is the one expressed in Virgil's phrase *facilis descensus Averno*: the movement which the devils when they first were driven into hell felt to be so contrary to their nature, but which now, as the inertia of original sin, drags all life downward to the grave. Creation began by segregating the principles of chaos into distinct elements or orders, in which like was attracted to like and remained aloof from the unlike. In the creation, particles of earth seek the sphere of earth, and so with the other elements: bubbles of air rise in water; springs of water rise in earth; fires go up; heavy objects in air fall to earth. This is still true, but after the fall Milton's personified Sin discovers a new kind of attraction of particles, a sort of moral gravitation:

> Or sympathy, or some connatural force,
> Powerful at greatest distance to unite
> With secret amity things of like kind
> By secretest conveyance.

We have been looking at some of the details of the vast symmetrical pattern in *Paradise Lost* in which evil parodies good. Some features in this pattern are very conspicuous: there is a council in hell in Book Two and a council in heaven in Book Three, each leading up to a volunteer: Christ journeys into chaos to create the world and Satan journeys into chaos to destroy it; Mammon builds Pandemonium in emulation of the City of God, and so on. Others are more difficult for the modern reader to see, especially those derived from the typological way of reading the Bible that Milton assumes to be second nature to his reader. The opening lines of the poem, with their reference to Moses' account of creation, lead us to expect that this is to be yet another creation poem like that of du Bartas, but instead the real creation is postponed until the beginning of the second half of the poem, and what we get immediately is a demonic parody of the creative process, as the devils in the deep begin to assume some order and coherence on relatively firm land. A demonic parody of the flood is included in the imagery, creation and flood being much the same phenomenon in the demonic world.

The same technique of dialectical parody comes into the

four great stages of redemption covered in Michael's summary
of the Bible. These, we remember, are the restoring of the
natural order with the end of the flood, the restoring of the
human order with the giving of the law to Israel, the Incarnation and the giving of the gospel to all mankind, and the final
apocalypse. The new creation of the world after the flood had
been anticipated in Christ's victory in heaven. The angels, like
twentieth-century man, carried their warfare to a point at
which the destruction of their world seemed imminent, but
Christ goes out to battle with the emblem of the rainbow, the
promise of indefinitely sustained life:

> Over their heads a crystal firmament,
> Whereon a sapphire throne, inlaid with pure
> Amber and colors of the showery arch.

And before long the order of nature is recreated in heaven as it
is later to be on earth:

> At his command the uprooted hills retired
> Each to his place; they heard his voice, and went
> Obsequious; Heaven his wonted face renewed,
> And with fresh flowerets hill and valley smiled.

On earth, the end of the flood is represented by the ark resting
on top of Ararat: this is immediately followed by the corresponding demonic image, the tower of Babel. The ark is
"smeared round with pitch," but the similar material of the
tower of Babel is more explicitly associated with the gun-
powder-plot imagery attached to the devils, as much of it
comes from

> The plain wherein a black bituminous gurge
> Boils out from underground, the mouth of Hell.

This dialectic is carried on in the Hebrew period, with such symbols as the "opprobrious hill" over against the temple of Solomon. The Hebrews made their unique contribution to history, as is the wont of human nature, through their least amiable characteristic: it was not the belief that their God was true but that all other gods were false which proved decisive for mankind. The conception "false god," hardly intelligible to a Greek or a Roman, is the conception that underlies Milton's wonderfully skilful counterpoint of biblical and Classical myth. With the coming of the gospel, however, the worship of the true God is no longer attached to a chosen nation, a holy land, a sacred city or temple, or anything locatable in time or space. The dialectic therefore sharpens into a kingdom not of this world, an invisible kingdom within the mind of man, as against the outward and visible kingdoms of this world, which are in Satan's keeping. The absoluteness of this dialectic is still, according to Milton, not always understood within the Christian church itself:

That church, that from the name of a distinct place takes authority to set up a distinct faith or government, is a schism and faction, not a church.

The most important event of the flood, as far as the imagery of *Paradise Lost* is concerned, is the washing away of Eden, the reason for which is, as Michael explains:

> To teach thee that God attributes to place
> No sanctity, if none be thither brought
> By men who there frequent or therein dwell.

But if Eden disappears as an outward environment, it revives as an inner state of mind, the "Paradise within thee, happier far" that Michael promises Adam. One of the first things that

Satan is compared to in the poem is the leviathan who looks like an island, but who would be likely to disappear into the water and drown the unlucky fisherman who landed on him. Eden disappears in the same way, but not so deceitfully. It is no good looking for Paradise anywhere on earth, but there is a garden inside the human mind, walled up and guarded by angels still, yet a place that the Word of God can open.

We are now perhaps in a position to see why Raphael's doubtful answer to Adam's questions takes up so much space in Book Eight. To assume that Milton is expressing an irritable obscurantism of his own through Raphael is the kind of assumption that it is never safe to make about Milton. When early critics expressed doubts whether the speeches of Satan were "blasphemous" or not, the answer is in the Renaissance conception of decorum, or appropriateness of the thing said to the character saying it. Of course they are blasphemous, and of course they ought to be. When Raphael blasphemes against our notion of the sacredness of free and unlimited intellectual enquiry, we ought to look first to see whether some principle of decorum is involved before ascribing the blasphemy to Milton himself.

If there is a personal aspect of Milton involved, it is of a very different kind. Milton has little sense of losing himself in an "O altitudo!" like Browne: mysteries, whether of faith or of reason, puzzle and bother him. For instance: the Genesis story speaks only of a serpent in Eden. It does not say that the serpent was a disguise for Satan: Milton got that interpretation from the New Testament. The cursing of the serpent is intelligible in the Genesis story, where the serpent himself is the agent of evil, but it is difficult to see why a harmless and helpless disguise should be cursed. Yet the cursing of the serpent is an unavoidable part of Milton's source, and must be dealt with somehow:

> Which when the Lord God heard, without delay
> To judgement he proceeded on th' accused
> Serpent, though brute, unable to transfer
> The guilt on him who made him instrument
> Of mischief, and polluted from the end
> Of his creation—justly then accursed,
> As vitiated in nature. More to know
> Concerned not Man (since he no further knew),
> Nor altered his offence; yet God at last
> To Satan, first in sin, his doom applied,
> Though in mysterious terms, judged as then best:
> And on the Serpent thus his curse let fall:—

Milton does not know why the serpent was cursed, and it is characteristic of a curious flat-footed honesty in Milton's mind that he should spread so obvious a bewilderment over a dozen lines of blank verse. It would be quite reasonable to assume that a similar bewilderment about what then seemed the paradoxes of the new Copernican astronomers should be reflected in Raphael's speech.

Adam has really two questions in his mind, though he does not get around to putting them both. First, is the universe geocentric? Second, if not, are there conscious beings in other heavenly bodies? For the earth is a heavenly body, seen from the higher Heaven as "Not unconform to other shining globes." What Raphael is saying is not that these questions are unanswerable, but that Adam should refrain from asking them. In front of him is a crucial test of his fidelity: in preparing for it he should concentrate on the Word of God within him and not on the works of God outside him. Whether the universe is geocentric or not in the eyes of God, there is no doubt that Adam's universe is for Adam. This is why Milton deliberately adopts a Ptolemaic onion-shaped cosmos for his poem, though, in contrast to Dante, he puts heaven and hell outside it. Adam already knows that there are other beings in other worlds—the angels in heaven—and the information has no bearing on the essential awareness he needs to prevent his being taken by surprise. His essential knowledge should be human-centred, practical, engaged knowledge. Adam may explore his world, but the most important thing for him to know is how to defend it. In *Areopagitica* Milton speaks of the high courage of those who will dispute of philosophical questions with the enemy at their very gates; but if they forgot the supreme duty of beating off the enemy, they could no longer be called courageous.

So with Adam. If he persists in obedience, nothing he wants to know is likely to be concealed from him; if he fails, there will be nothing in the whole universe outside him to help him. When Michael comes to earth in Book Eleven, his descent is associated, in the last Classical allusion in *Paradise Lost*, with Hermes putting Argus to sleep with his "opiate rod." The image of the hundred eyes closing down as Adam settles into his new perception of time and space gives us some notion of how extensive a paradise he has lost. We can understand, in passing, why Milton was attracted to the doctrine of mortalism, that human souls sleep until the Last Judgment. Not until history has ended can there be a new paradisal place.

There is only one historical figure outside the Bible who is explicitly and repeatedly alluded to in *Paradise Lost*, and that is Galileo. Such prominence is an impressive tribute to Milton's sense of his importance, and, perhaps, to Milton's own insight in grasping that importance. The references to Galileo are by no means hostile, and it is clear from the use made of him in the argument of *Areopagitica* that in Milton's ideal state he would be a highly respected citizen. But if they are not hostile they are curiously deprecatory. Milton seems to regard Galileo, most inaccurately, as concerned primarily with the question of whether the heavenly bodies, more particularly the moon, are habitable—as a pioneer of science fiction rather than of science. As Satan hoists his great shield, the shield, in a glancing parody of the shield of Achilles which depicted mainly a world at peace, is associated with Galileo peering through his telescope at the moon:

> to descry new lands,
> Rivers or mountains in her spotty globe.

Galileo thus appears to symbolize, for Milton, the gaze outward on physical nature, as opposed to the concentration inward on human nature, the speculative reason that searches for new places, rather than the moral reason that tries to create a new state of mind.

The symbolic Galileo in Milton thus resembles the later symbolic Newton in Blake: he stands for a philosophical vision that, in Marx's famous phrase, thinks it more important to study the world than to change it. For fallen man, rooted in the demonic perception of the universe, the form of God's creation has been entirely replaced by space, and while he may hope, like Satan, that space may produce or disclose new worlds, there is nothing divine in space that man can *now* see, nothing to afford him a model of the new world he must construct within himself. Of course he will find reason and design in the world, but no further than the rational power with which he perceives it. The Galileo vision in Milton sees man as a spectator of a theatrical nature, and such a vision is opposed to the vision of human liberty. It is not idolatrous in itself, but the demonic basis of it is. The vision of liberty pulls away from the world and attaches itself to the total human body within, the Word that reveals the Eden in the redeemable human soul, and so releases the power that leads to a new heaven and a new earth.

Children of God
and Nature

IN THE SOUL OF MAN, as God originally created it, there is a hierarchy. This hierarchy has three main levels: the reason, which is in control of the soul; the will, the agent carrying out the decrees of the reason, and the appetite. Reason and will, the decree and the act, are related in man much as the Father and the Son are related in the Godhead. The will is never free in the sense of being autonomous or detached from some other aspect of the soul, but when reason is in charge of the soul the will is free because it participates in the freedom of the reason. In one of his academic Prolusions Milton says, as an axiom generally accepted: "the human intellect, as head and ruler, surpasses in splendor the other faculties of the mind; it governs and illuminates with its splendor the will itself, otherwise blind and dark, that like the moon shines with another's light."

The appetite is subordinate to both, and is controlled by the will from the reason. Of the appetites two are of central importance: the appetite for food and the sexual appetite. Both of these are part of the divine creation, and are therefore good. Even so, it is curious how emphatic Milton is about food as an element of both paradisal and heavenly life. In the unfallen world eating has something sacramental about it: Raphael explains how it is part of the upward movement in nature back toward its Creator, and even the form in which food is provided indicates the "providence" behind it:

> The savoury pulp they chew, and in the rind,
> Still as they thirsted, scoop the brimming stream.

The angels also eat and drink "in communion sweet," and Milton insists that, whatever the theologians may say, Raphael really ate the fruit salad provided for him by Eve. Not only does he eat it but he explains how he ate it. He appears to have no excretory organs except the pores of his skin—if angels have skin—but at any rate the upper end of his food pipe has been implanted in him by the Deity.

Milton also insists, again referring to objecting theologians, that sexual intercourse existed between Adam and Eve before the fall. There remains of course only the fourth question, the sexual life of angels, the subject of some curious speculations later on by Swedenborg. We are told that spirits can assume either sex, which seems to imply that sex has some point even in a spiritual nature. Adam's natural curiosity, combined with other elements we shall look at in a moment, prompts him to ask Raphael a direct question on this point. The question, not unnaturally, is not directly answered, but when it is asked Raphael blushes, mutters something about having just remembered another appointment, and bustles off. He does not leave however until he has given Adam a very strong hint what the answer is:

> Let it suffice thee that thou know'st
> Us happy, and without Love no happiness.
> Whatever pure thou in the body enjoy'st
> (And pure thou wert created) we enjoy
> In eminence, and obstacle find none
> Of membrane, joint, or limb, exclusive bars.

Or, as Blake was to say in a tone more ribald than either Milton's or Swedenborg's:

> in Eternity
> Embracings are comminglings from the head even to the feet,
> And not a pompous high priest entering by a secret place.

There is a rough but useful correspondence between the hierarchy of reason, will and appetite in the individual and the social hierarchy of men, women and children that would have developed in Eden if Adam had not fallen. In this analogy the man would correspond to the level of the reason, the woman to that of the will united to the reason, and the child to that of the appetite, subordinate to both but still protected and cherished. We cannot prove this directly, as no unfallen society ever developed, but it seems implicit in Milton's argument. We are told that even in heaven there is such a thing as seniority, and when Satan disguises himself as a stripling cherub he makes all the deference to seniority toward Uriel that a young cherub ought to make, though how there could be young and old cherubim in eternity is not explained. The supremacy of husband over wife is taken for granted by Milton because he found it in the New Testament. When Milton says of Adam and Eve: "He for God only, she for God in him" he is merely putting a Pauline doctrine into pentameter verse. The correspondence of reason and will with man and woman is marked in the beginning of Book Nine, when Eve wants to go and work by herself and Adam allows her to go. Adam is right in doing so because he is leaving her will free, while retaining the natural supremacy of his own reason. He goes wrong only in accepting her (by then perverted) advice in connection with his own decision.

As far as the present world is concerned, we should remember something that many readers of Milton are apt to forget, that the authority of husband over wife is spiritual authority only. No man, except a man living entirely by the light of the gospel, would have the kind of integrity of which such an authority would be a by-product, nor could a woman who did not have a corresponding integrity be capable of responding to it. A bullying or dictatorial attitude toward one's wife would be merely one more example of what Milton calls man's effeminate slackness. Many theologians have asserted that the wife ought to be in subjection to her husband because woman brought sin into the world, but this is arguing directly from the unfallen to the fallen state, something Milton never does. Milton does say in *The Christian Doctrine* that the authority of the husband was increased after the fall, but this is an empirical observation on the patriarchal narratives in the Old Testament, not a deduction from the Eden story.

It is understandable however that Milton should see in the cult of courtly love, of *Frauendienst* or worship of women in the literary conventions of his time, one of the most direct and eloquent symbolic results of the fall of man. For this reason, Milton places the supremacy of Eve over Adam at the central point of the fall itself. "Was she thy God?" the real God asks

Adam. As soon as Eve has eaten of the apple she becomes jealous of Adam, that is, her love for Adam is immediately perverted into jealousy, and jealousy is essentially a feeling of possessiveness. She feels that unless she can preserve some kind of power over Adam she will not be his equal, or "perhaps"

> —A thing not undesirable—sometime
> Superior; for, inferior, who is free?

echoing as she says this the argument of Satan himself, who can only understand ruling and serving, and prefers reigning in hell to serving in heaven. So Eve brings about Adam's fall by making him feel that he cannot live without her and that he must remain with her even at the price of dying with her or of being under her sway indefinitely.

We may understand in the light of this principle of perverted female supremacy one of the puzzling episodes in the dialogue between Raphael and Adam. At the end of Book Eight, Adam attempts to explain to Raphael something of the feeling which Eve has inspired in him, and he speaks of these feelings as a kind of adoration or awe. He feels that there is something about Eve that creates a mystery, and hints at a kind of reality beyond what his own reason shows him:

> Greatness of mind and nobleness their seat
> Build in her loveliest, and create an awe
> About her, as a guard angelic placed.

Raphael does not know that Adam has just used, by ironic anticipation, the image of Paradise after he has been excluded from it. But he does know that something is very wrong, and in his anxiety to put it right he goes too far. He rebukes Adam in a way that Adam finds baffling, and his speech ends with what Adam must have found, in the context, an insensitively coarse remark:

> Not sunk in carnal pleasure; for which cause
> Among the beasts no mate for thee was found.

Adam is said to be "half" abashed by this; he is, as nearly as anyone can be in an unfallen state, shocked and angered. Yet what Raphael has been too anxious to correct does in fact turn out to be the cause of Adam's fall. The supremacy of Adam over Eve is the free and human relation; the supremacy of Eve could soon become a road leading to intellectual enslavement.

Milton's argument for divorce is really an argument for annulment, that is, an argument that if the relations between man and woman are intolerable, no marriage, in the gospel sense, has really taken place. The marriage Jesus describes as indissoluble is a lifetime companionship that can be consummated, or finished, only by the death of one of the partners. The union of Adam and Eve in Eden is the pattern of such a marriage, but not every legalized sex act in the fallen world achieves that pattern. But the argument for annulment really resolves itself into an argument against idolatry. The man has the right to divorce his wife (or the wife the husband) if she is a threat to his spiritual integrity, and she cannot be that without representing something of what idolatry means to Milton. When Eve, after her fall, comes to Adam and urges him to fall with her, that is the point at which Adam should have "divorced" Eve, hence the argument for divorce comes into the very act of the fall itself.

Few can have read *Paradise Lost* without being struck by the curiously domesticated nature of the life of Adam and Eve

in Eden before the fall. Adam and Eve are suburbanites in the
nude, and like other suburbanites they are preoccupied with
gardening, with their own sexual relations, and with the details
of their rudimentary housekeeping. Even what many would
now regard as the horrors of suburban life are only delights to
Adam and Eve. They do not mind that they are constantly
under inspection by angelic neighbours, or by God himself,
for, says Milton, "they thought no ill." Such extraordinary
trustfulness is a natural part of the state of innocence. There's
an angel up in the sky. So there is: how nice; perhaps he'll stay
to lunch. And when Eve serves the meal, goes away and leaves
the men to their masculine conversation, we feel that we are
as close as Paradise can get to port and cigars. Commentators
on Milton, at least since Taine a century ago, have said everything on this point that needs to be said. But the prevailing
assumption has been that all this represents unconscious humour
on the part of a humourless poet, and this assumption is quite
wrong.

It is essential to Milton's argument to present Adam and Eve
in this way. For it is Milton's belief that the original state of
man was civilized, and that it was far closer to the average life
of a seventeenth-century Englishman than it was to that of a
noble savage. Savagery and primitivism came later, and were
never intended by God to be part of man's life. Further, it
would be a mistake to imagine, as the hasty reader often does,
that because Adam and Eve are unfallen and sinless they must
necessarily be insipid. They are not insipid at all, but lively,
even explosive personalities. Adam has not been in the world
five minutes before he is arguing with his Maker and pointing
out to him the deficiencies of a life in which there is no other

human being. This amuses his Creator, but it pleases him too to feel that there is so instant a response from the reason which he has planted in Adam's mind. When Raphael rebukes Adam, as Adam feels, unjustly, Adam makes a shrewd flanking attack by way of his question about Raphael's sex life, and on the way mentions in a parenthesis that he is sticking to his own views and is not allowing any angel to bully him out of them:

> Though higher of the genial bed by far,
> And with mysterious reverence, I deem.

Let us return to the episode in Book Nine in which we are told that Eve has suddenly taken it into her head to go and do her pruning by herself. Adam makes a long speech, in impeccable blank verse, pointing out that, as they are about to be assailed by a clever and ruthless enemy, it might be better for them to stay together and not separate. Eve says that that is very true, and that she would like to go off and prune by herself. Adam makes another long speech, in equally impeccable blank verse, making the same point with elaborations. Eve says that all that is very true, and that she will now go off and prune by herself. At this point Adam attempts the manœuvre which so many husbands have attempted, of trying to get the last word by telling her to go and do as she likes:

> Go in thy native innocence; rely
> On what thou hast of virtue; summon all;
> For God towards thee hath done his part: do thine.
> So spake the Patriarch of Mankind; but Eve
> Persisted; yet submiss, though last, replied.

This unfallen spat indicates that there is room for explosive personalities in Paradise, because there is no malice in their explosion. Similarly with the liveliness of intellect that they display. When Eve has a troubling dream, and does not understand its meaning, Adam, who is several hours older, explains to her the origin of dreams, how they operate, and what their machinery is. The speech is intended to convey the sense of the freshness of discovery, not of the staleness of opinion.

The same applies to the kind of language they use, the language which has often puzzled readers and been ridiculed by them. Adam and Eve use the kind of stylized hierarchic language which indicates their exuberance in the possession of language as a new and fresh form of intellectual energy. The formality of their speeches is verbal play, and reflects the exuberance with which Milton himself, in addressing his own language in his early *Vacation Exercise* poem, described the appropriate epic diction:

> Such as may make thee search thy coffers round,
> Before thou clothe my fancy in fit sound.

Such formal rhetoric is at the opposite pole of human life from the dialogue in a Hemingway novel, which is equally appropriate to its purpose because it represents a weariness with human speech. Such communication, where nothing really needs to be said, is a parody of the kind of communication which according to Raphael the angels have, and which is intuitive rather than discursive. Adam and Eve are simply enjoying the possession of the power of discursive communication.

After the fall, the hierarchy implanted by God in the human soul is not merely upset, but reversed. Appetite now moves into the top place in the human soul, and by doing so it ceases to be appetite and is transformed into passion, the drive toward death. The appetites are a part of the creation, and like every other part of the creation they are an energy which seeks its fulfilment in form. Hunger is specifically satisfied with food, and the sexual desire by sexual intercourse. When appetite is perverted into passion, the drives of sex and hunger are preverted into lust and greed. Passion operates in the mind as though it were an external force, compelling the soul to obey against its own best interests, and the passions of greed and lust have two qualities that the appetites do not have: excess and mechanical energy. Hunger can be satisfied by food, but greed cannot be satisfied by anything: it seeks an excess of food, and when it runs out of food, it will seek to acquire other things out of mechanical habit. Eve is hungry before she eats the forbidden fruit, greedy immediately afterward, and her greed runs on into a desire to possess Adam.

After Adam has fallen with her, sexual intercourse between them is resumed, but this time its basis is entirely different. It is not the expression of the love of Adam for Eve, but rather the generalized and mechanical expression of the lust of a man for a woman, the woman being Eve because she is the only woman within reach. The will is now the agent of passion instead of reason, for the will must be the agent of one or the other. The behaviour of mankind takes on that mechanical and amorphous quality which Milton describes in chaos: he speaks elsewhere of the futility of efforts to define sin, "to put a girdle about that chaos." This inversion of the human mind, with passion on top and will its agent, reduces reason to the lowest point in the soul, where it is normally a helpless critic of what the passion is doing, able to point out the correct course, but, in the passion-driven mind, powerless to affect its decisions for long.

What happens in the human individual happens by analogy in fallen human society. Passion acts as though it were an external force, a tyrant of the mind, and a society made up of passionate individuals becomes a tyranny, in which the tyrant is the embodiment of the self-enslavement of his victims, as Michael explains to Adam:

> Reason in Man obscured, or not obeyed,
> Immediately inordinate desires
> And upstart passions catch the government
> From reason, and to servitude reduce
> Man, till then free. Therefore, since he permits
> Within himself unworthy powers to reign
> Over free reason, God, in judgement just,
> Subjects him from without to violent lords,
> Who oft as undeservedly enthrall
> His outward freedom.

Usually we have a secular tyrant and a spiritual tyrant or priest. The latter, in Christianity, is what Milton means by a prelate, a person who exerts temporal power in what ought to be the area of spiritual authority. Under the tyrant and the priest and their followers come the victims, the general public, and under them again come the few people equipped with enough reason to protest against what is happening and to try to rouse the conscience of the very small number who can be persuaded to agree and act with them. This is the situation of which the archetype is Abdiel among the rebel angels, which is also, as explained, the archetype of human heroism.

The distinction between lust and greed is that lust is a vice turned outward and affecting other people; greed is a vice that turns inward and affects oneself. These two forms of tyranny produce what for Milton are the two infallible signs of a perverted church: inquisition and indulgence, the desire to suppress freedom of thought and the tendency to provide easy formulas for the less dangerous vices. The former develops the censor who is attacked in *Areopagitica*; the latter develops what Milton calls the "hireling." Among the pamphlets written on the eve of the Restoration, the first two deal with these two forms of religious perversion. *A Treatise of Civil Power in Ecclesiastical Causes* is concerned mainly with the separation of spiritual and temporal authority necessary to avoid what Milton calls in *Areopagitica* "the laziness of a licensing church"; *The Likeliest Means to Remove Hirelings* is concerned with the complementary problem.

If we look at the visions which Michael shows Adam in Book Eleven, between the murder of Abel and the flood, we may be puzzled to find that some of them are not biblical. The story of Cain and Abel is naturally the first vision, and this story centres on one of Milton's central emblems, the altar of acceptable sacrifice, along with its demonic parody. This is followed by a vision of a lazar-house, the victims of which are said to have brought many of their evils on themselves by intemperance in eating and drinking, in other words by greed. We get a somewhat prosaic homily on the virtue of temperance at this point, yet the reason for it is clear: Milton is trying to define the origin of greed in the human body and its excessive appetite. The vision of the lazar-house is followed by another based on those mysterious verses in Genesis about the sons of God who discovered that the daughters of women were fair. The sons of God, according to Milton, were virtuous men and the daughters of women were daughters of women. The gigantic results of their union illustrate the physical origin of lust in the human body. These two visions are followed by two others, one of a cattle raid and one of a scene of riotous and drunken festivity. These two scenes are war and peace as they are usually understood in human life, war as a direct product of human greed, and "peace," that is, luxury, as a direct product of human lust. These four antediluvian scenes thus make up a vision of greed and lust spilling excessively and mechanically over all human life in a moral flood of which the physical one seems the only possible outcome.

On the demonic level, lust and greed become the two forms of vice which have traditionally been classified as force and fraud, the ethical basis on which Dante divides sins in his *Inferno*. Force and fraud are the outstanding characteristics of the devils as they are revealed in the council in Book Two. First we have Moloch speaking in favour of a renewed assault on heaven. We note again the perverted qualities of appetite, excess and mechanical repetition. Moloch appears to be someone of considerable courage—at any rate he has more of it than most of the other devils have—but if there is anything to be said for Plato's conception of courage as the knowledge of what is formidable, then Moloch, lacking any such knowledge, does not have genuine courage. What he has would better be described as ferocity. He is followed by Belial, who has the astuteness and wiliness that Moloch lacks, and who tries to persuade the devils to caution. Just as Moloch appears to have courage, so Belial appears to have prudence; but what he really has is sloth or indolence: again he has no knowledge of

what is formidable, only of what is inconvenient. The force of
Moloch is lust in action, an outward-directed destructive
power; the fraud of Belial is an inward-directed slothfulness,
greedily clutching its "intellectual being."

Moloch and Belial are followed by Mammon, who represents evil in the aspect that we have already met so often in
Milton, as a parody of good. It is Mammon who sets up in hell
a close parody of the City of God, which is golden like that
city, though a different kind of gold. Mammon corresponds
in the human society to Nimrod, who sets up both the tower
of Babel and a systematic tyranny as a part of human life, and
who succeeds to the ferocity and indolence of antediluvian
life. Mammon is followed by Beelzebub, and Beelzebub
suggests the consolidation of all three preceding views of evil,
in the form of an attack on heaven which falls just short of
heaven. Satan undertakes the voyage through chaos to realize
this combination of force, fraud and parody of good; and when
he gets to the slippery edge of nothing, the outer shell of the
primum mobile, just beside the gate of heaven, Milton treats us
to a curious digression. There is nothing here at this point, but
later on, in human history, this area is that of the Limbo of
Vanities, where a number of characters whom he itemizes in
some detail find themselves sprawling after death. The people
who arrive in the Limbo of Vanities are of two kinds: they are
the people who have tried to take the kingdom of heaven
either by force or by fraud. The former are those who have
committed suicide in order to reach heaven; the latter are
hypocrites who have tried to disguise themselves. It is poetically
right that, when Satan is in prospect of the end of his journey,

he should meet there what is symbolically the goal of the human beings who are coming up from the opposite direction: again an attack on heaven that falls just short of heaven.

The hierarchy in the soul of man is, however, more complicated than this threefold structure of reason, will and appetite. Reason is subordinate to a higher principle than itself: revelation, coming directly from the Word of God, which emancipates and fulfils the reason and gives it a basis to work on which the reason could not achieve by itself. The point at which revelation impinges on reason is the point at which discursive understanding begins to be intuitive: the point of the emblematic vision or parable, which is the normal unit in the teaching of Jesus. The story of the fall of Satan is a parable to Adam, giving him the kind of knowledge he needs in the only form appropriate to a free man. We are speaking here of knowledge as received: for the poet, who has brought his poetic gifts into line with revelation, the same point would be the point of inspiration. Milton does not have exactly the later Romantic conception of imagination, but Keats was right in seeing in Adam's dream the corresponding conception, a mental image that becomes a reality:

> Each tree
> Loaden with fairest fruit, that hung to the eye
> Tempting, stirred in me sudden appetite
> To pluck and eat; whereat I waked, and found
> Before mine eyes all real, as the dream
> Had lively shadowed.

Here the dream is of food in its sacramental form, the provision of God of which the forbidden fruit is, once again, the demonic parody.

Below the appetite, similarly, there is the parody of revelation, the fancy or fantasy, the aspect of the mind that is expressed in dreams, including daydreams, and which has the quality of illuminating the appetite from below, as revelation illuminates the reason from above. This fancy is represented by the corresponding dream of Eve. The occasion of her dream was Satan whispering in her ear; but the dream itself, in its manifest content, was a Freudian wish-fulfilment dream. She finds herself in front of the forbidden tree and eating its fruit, thereby gratifying her hunger; the modern reader cannot help noticing that the dream involves flying, and so is a sexual dream as well. The explanation of the dream given her by Adam, at least the explanation of it as a physical process, is based on the conception of three levels of "spirits," vegetative, cordial and intellectual, the spirits in the body being the point at which the physical substance is transmuted into a spiritual one. Dreams are produced by a premature uprush of vegetative spirits from the lower parts of the body, which is their natural habitat, into the brain. This process in Eve is thus a microscopic example of the upward demonic explosive movement, from chaos into order, dealt with previously.

When the soul of man is reversed in the fall, this fantasy is now on top, illuminating the passion. In this perverted situation it is the force which Milton always associates with idolatry, the demonic emblematic vision. Idolatry in *Paradise Lost* is specifically associated with the forbidden tree. As soon as Eve has eaten the forbidden fruit, she bows to the tree and does it homage: that act is the beginning and end of all idolatry in the human mind. Idolatry in human history is of course the work of the devils, but the devils are involved in idolatry too, and we are told that every so often, in hell, they are compelled to climb up the branches of a tree which Milton describes as an "illusion," and eat the fruit of that tree, fruit which, like the apples of Sodom, is fair outside but dust and ashes inside. The devils cannot inspire idolatry without becoming idols themselves: once again we have the biblical judgment on idols: "They that make them are like unto them." This identification with the evil that one creates is also symbolized by the variety of disguises that Satan assumes. Milton speaks of him as "Squat, like a toad, close at the ear of Eve," as perching on the tree of life "like a cormorant," as moving through the garden "like a black mist." He is not saying that Satan actually took these forms: he merely wants the reader to visualize them in connection with Satan. Similarly, when Satan tries on various animals for size before settling on the serpent, including the lion and the tiger, he is anticipating the later fallen forms of these animals, when they become beasts of prey.

In the genuine fallen human mind, where reason lies at the bottom, a helpless critic of the passion above it, reason, in those who trust to it, may also be illuminated from below in a genuine way, by the power of prophecy, by the revelation which is transmitted to mankind through the scriptures and other agents of divine revelation. Here again Adam and Eve, after their fall, represent complementary forms of such illumination: Adam receives the prophecy of Michael later fulfilled in the scriptures; Eve is visited by unitemized but clearly consoling dreams.

We notice that Eve from the beginning is a more remote and withdrawn character than Adam: in a fallen state, therefore, Eve is more susceptible to greed, and Adam to lust, taking these words in the expanded sense that we have been using them in, as introverted and extroverted vice respectively. The first time we meet Eve, in the chronological sequence, she is looking at her reflection in the water, an image which would suggest to the contemporary reader of Milton the story of Narcissus, interpreted in the mythological handbooks as an emblem of pride and as the Classical equivalent of the story of the fall of man. However, Eve is not narcissistic at this point: she merely feels that her own reflection in the water is very pleasant, and when Adam comes along her first feeling about him is that he is not quite up to her own standard of attractiveness. Her state of mind is not pride but the kind of vanity that we find amusing and disarming, and so innocent. This is the basis in her mind on which Satan is able to work. After her dream, she remains quiet and reserved through the next day, and we notice her action in slipping away unobtrusively from the company of Adam and Raphael. The next morning the same feeling persists in her unaccountable desire to be by herself. Satan then comes to her, disguised as a talking snake, and holds her attention by the fact that he can talk. She does not hear a word he is saying, beyond a general notion that she is being flattered, nor does he intend her to. He wants only to keep her fascinated by the image of the talking snake, while everything he says gets past the guard of her consciousness and falls into the depths of what we should now call her subconscious. What he says thereby instils in her the notion of her own individuality, somebody in her own right, herself and not merely an appendage to Adam or to God. When he leads her to the tree of knowledge and she hesitates before it, she searches her own mind to see what her state of mind is. What she finds there, of course, is Satan's speech, which has got into her mind without her noticing it, and she repeats Satan's arguments as though they were her own.

As soon as she has eaten of the forbidden tree, heaven, which has previously been inside her, part of the community she is attached to, then separates from her and goes up into the sky, becoming something remote and external. She is immediately possessed by the idea of secrecy which is a part of shame: "And I perhaps am secret: heaven is high." With the sense of secrecy comes the sense of resentment, because God is no longer inside her as part of her own conscience, but somewhere outside her watching her with a censorious eye: "Our great Forbidder, safe with all his spies." Thus her love for Adam, turning as it does into jealousy, becomes a desire to have Adam as an appendage to herself:

> This may be well; but what if God have seen,
> And death ensue? Then I shall be no more;
> And Adam, wedded to another Eve,
> Shall live with her enjoying, I extinct!
> A death to think!

This is as sombre a depth of irony as Milton reaches in the entire poem. Eve does not so much mind dying: the real death is the thought of Adam surviving with another woman. This is the state into which Adam also falls, and there follow consequently the psychological changes of the fall in his mind too. This ends in a vicious quarrel between the two, all the more terrifying because so petty, and the last line of Book Nine is: "And of their vain contest appeared no end." With the words "no end," suddenly the sense of the fate of the devils in hell opens out and one glimpses the possibility of Adam and Eve snarling at each other to all eternity, which of course is what they would do if there were no redemption in the world.

At the same time, Adam is motivated by his desire to live with Eve and his feeling that he cannot live without her. Conceptually and theologically, he is entirely wrong, and we have explained how he should have "divorced" Eve at the moment of her fall. But again, the conceptual and theological situation is not the dramatic one. Adam's decision to die with Eve rather than live without her impresses us, in our fallen state, as a heroic decision. We feel a certain nobility in what Adam does: Eve also feels this and expresses it. When Adam falls, he falls, as Milton says, "Against his better knowledge, not deceived," but he also attracts some sympathy from a reader who feels that if Adam had actually gone back to God accusing Eve of mortal sin and demanding to be released from his contract with her he would have forfeited that sympathy. The reader feels that, whether or not this is the right thing for Adam to do, this is what he himself might well have done if he had been in Adam's place. And that, of course, is exactly Milton's point.

This sense of a contrast between the dramatic and the conceptual aspects of a situation is there because it fits the Christian myth, yet it follows Classical precedent too. In Homer, Odysseus gets our sympathy by preferring his mortal wife Penelope to the immortality promised him by Calypso. Much closer to Milton, however, is the account of Dido in Virgil. Virgil is a Roman poet writing for Roman readers, and certainly both Virgil and his readers recognized the call of a higher destiny for Aeneas. Obviously he had to get away from the Carthaginian Dido to Italy and found Rome. Yet, when

Aeneas meets Dido in the lower world, Dido walks off with all the dramatic honours of the situation. What poor Aeneas gets is not only an annihilating snub, but the deadliest insult that any woman can give her faithless lover, as she turns contemptuously away and goes off to look for her husband.

The Dido episode in Virgil is a romantic episode, and the sense of the romantic in the relations of Adam, and Eve after their fall is centrally important. We are aware at once of the inscrutability of the fallen soul, the sense of the self-enclosed ego or individual remote and cut off from every other form of individual. Along with this goes the sense of melancholy. Book Nine of *Paradise Lost* is, as already suggested, among other things a wonderful cultural anticipation of the eighteenth-century cult of the noble savage. As soon as Adam falls, he loses his sense of humour, a fact indicated by his speech to Eve, which is full of puns, like the speeches of the devils after they have discovered artillery. The reason why Milton associates punning with a sinful nature will be discussed in the last chapter. In any case, the sense of melancholy and of a somewhat precarious dignity, the wrong kind of dignity that cannot survive the first banana-peeling, so to speak, is the psychological basis of the tyrannical and perverted form of human society that is going to become established in the place where Eden was. These are also products of shame, the feeling of being withdrawn from the city of light, of which Adam is a member because he lives in one of its greenest suburbs. He is now plunged into a sense of human life as something that begins anew with each individual, where each individual is the centre of his own universe, removed from everyone else and communicating only with the greatest difficulty, aware of the existence of other people only because reluctantly forced to be. This is the quality of melancholy which seems to Milton characteristic of primitive life, its root the kind of pathos that results from being cut off from one's community. Romanticism continues into the tenth book, where Adam and Eve go through a *Liebestod* stage of a suicide pact, then outgrow the longing to die with each other and advance into the stage of longing to die for each other. This is the point at which the human race becomes, from God's point of view, something worth redeeming.

The human fall parallels the previously described demonic one. When Satan rebels against God, he loses his status in his community. He is therefore like a hand cut off from the body, which has no purpose or usefulness or life in itself once it has become severed from the organism of which it forms part. So Satan's discovery of his own separated ego, which at the first moment of this discovery was so exhilarating, very soon becomes a psychological imprisonment. He finds himself walled in by the jail of his individuality, so that, as he points out, he would create a hell even if he were replaced in heaven. We notice that the devils, unlike man, cannot die. Man is excluded from Paradise after he has eaten of the tree of knowledge in order to prevent him from reaching for the tree of life. God fears his doing this, not because he is jealous for his own privileges, although the Genesis wording seems to suggest this and Milton echoes it, but to prevent man from living forever in a fallen world. The latter is the fate of the devils: the devils cannot die because they cannot make the act of surrender involved in death: hence what they have is a kind of parody of immortality. They are not really immortal; they are merely undying. And although Milton was compelled to keep the doctrine of eternal punishment for sinful human beings in his theological structure, *Paradise Lost* is a poem with no relish of damnation in it: this theme is, as nearly as possible, eliminated.

It has been said that a great portrait gives us the feeling that the back of the head has been as solidly realized as the visible parts. If we knew nothing of Milton except *Paradise Lost*, we should still be aware that the structure was supported by a powerful and coherent skeleton of ideas: when we turn to the prose writings these ideas come more clearly into view. Some of them may be called commonplaces, except that when they become integral to Milton's outlook they cease to be commonplaces. And while there are certainly major changes of emphasis between *Areopagitica* and *Paradise Lost*, there is nothing in *Paradise Lost* which is really a denying or a going back on the great issues he had fought for. In any case these issues, so far as the student of Milton is interested in them, are not prefabricated ones: they are issues articulated by Milton himself, as part of that encyclopaedic range of ideas which the epic expresses.

One of the main constructs elaborated from the Bible in later Christian thought is that of the different levels of civilization, as we have it in St. Augustine's conception of the City of God and its relations with the church on earth, the Roman power, and the *civitas terrena*. In Milton, where so much of the action takes place before human history begins, much of the symbolism has to be anticipatory. The significant acts of the Son of God prefigure his acts in the Incarnation: the expulsion of the devils prefigures the cleansing of the temple, and the silencing of chaos his command of the Sea of Galilee. Similarly, the devils in Book One are associated by anticipation with the two aspects of civilization that they later introduce to human life, tyranny and anarchy. Tyranny is represented in the Bible more particularly by Egypt and Babylon, and in Book One the imagery links the devils with the plagues of Egypt, the drowning of "Busiris and his Memphian chivalry," and the gorgeous temples in "Babylon and great Alcairo." Anarchy Milton associates with the *Völkerwanderung* at the fall of the Roman Empire, and in later books with the nomadic tribes of Scythia and Great Tartary, a movement repeating that of the flood spilling over human life. The entry of Sin and Death into fallen nature is linked to the great host of Xerxes, attempting "the liberty of Greece to yoke," when Xerxes scourged the sea (which ought to have been his ally, being a symbol of chaos) as a traitor to his cause.

Above tyranny is the condition of law, represented by the Hebrews and, in a different context, by the brief periods of "ancient liberty" in Greece and Rome. Tyranny is an externally imposed discipline, and in law there is a principle of inward discipline. The law in itself is concerned only with the outward consequences of actions: as far as the law is concerned, anyone not actually convicted of stealing is an honest man. Hence the primary function of the law is to define the thief, to "discover sin," as Michael says. To the criminal, society becomes tyrannical: justice is the internal condition of the just man, but the external antagonist of the criminal, and so acts as an externally compelling force on him. But that very fact indicates that the honest man must have a higher standard of morality than the mere fear of getting caught, and while the law cannot define honesty as it can define theft, the honest man still knows what it is. What the law cannot do is to make people honest. Yet there is a principle of order and stability, and consequently of freedom, in law, and a morally sound society, whether within Christianity or outside it, is capable of achieving freedom, though never for long enough to make the gospel unnecessary.

The Mosaic code provides a complete moral law, yet Milton does not associate it, as he does the republics of Greece and Rome, with liberty: he thinks of it in Pauline terms as a bondage from which the gospel has released us. Mosaic law is partly ceremonial, and so more constraining than moral law alone would be, yet it is a higher gift than moral law, because it prevents morality from becoming an end in itself. Its meaning is typological, the acts it enjoins being symbols of the spiritual truths of the gospel. Hence it corresponds in society to what we have called the emblematic vision in the individual, the point at which reason begins to comprehend revelation. As a series of acts, arbitrary in themselves but deriving their meaning from a higher kind of truth, the ceremonial law sets up a force in society that might be called counter-idolatry. The prohibition not to make gods in the image of man, or nature, may lead, if only as "types and shadows," to understanding that man is the image of God. Hence the gospel can succeed the Mosaic law, as its inevitable fulfilment, in a way that it cannot fulfil the enlightened virtue of the heathen.

The gospel sets one free from the law, but of course one does not become free of the law by breaking the law, only more tangled up with it than ever. What the gospel does is to internalize the law, to remove every aspect of it that acts as an external compulsion. Liberty is thus the same thing as inner necessity. If an artist painting a picture knows exactly what he is doing, every brush stroke is compelled because it is free. If someone learning to play the piano is still hesitating and exercising his freedom of will about playing the right notes, he is not playing very well. He can only set himself free to play the piano when he has compelled himself to play automatically the right notes. Similarly with the ethical nature: the person who is free is simply incapable of stealing or lying. The gospel's moral demands in fact are so rigorous that the law, which is far more tolerant, is compelled to remain where it is: it would produce the most fantastic tyranny to try to make a new law out of the gospel. Milton was attracted by the topic of divorce because for him the legal obstacles to divorce had been derived from the teachings of Jesus, and the law has to be in accord with Moses, not with Jesus. In society the gospel exerts a spiritual authority, the power of persuasion inspired by good example. It has no soldiers and no magistrates. The law is represented by temporal authority, which does have soldiers and magistrates, and ought to realize the limitations of what such apparatus can do.

Liberty for Milton is not something that starts with man: it starts with God. It is not something that man naturally wants for himself, but something that God is determined he shall have; man cannot want it unless he is in a regenerate state, prepared to accept the inner discipline and responsibility that go with it. Hence, as Milton says, none can love freedom but good men; the rest want not freedom but licence. When a "licentious" man says he wants liberty, what he really wants is mastery, or lust. If he cannot get mastery, he will give the name liberty to greed, to the querulous desire to be left alone with his pleasanter vices. If he cannot achieve that, he will identify liberty with its demonic parody, a glad acceptance of slavery, proceeding from the influence of Moloch and Belial to that of Mammon.

The knowledge of good and evil which Adam acquired in his fall is knowledge in which evil is primary and good a secondary derivation from evil. Mercy and peace, in this world, are goods which mean that someone has already been cruel or that a war has stopped. This is why temporal authority can never be an end in itself, and why its agents cannot deal with the gospel. Moral law can only define the lawbreaker: it cannot distinguish what is above the law from what is below it, the prophet from the criminal, Jesus from Barabbas. This is the position of the censor as attacked in *Areopagitica,* who finds the prophet as subversive as the genuine traitor. Revelation comes from an infinite mind to a finite one; there can be no definitive human understanding of revelation, and consequently revelation is always addressed to a fundamentally unwilling and resisting audience. The desire to persecute has its origin, not in zeal, but in the deification of some human form of understanding: its root is not "You must believe in God," but "You must believe in what I mean by God."

The society produced by the gospel is the church, and the church is a community whose members have all been made free and equal by their faith. The natural image for this community is the square or cube, probably the shape of the City of God, and certainly that of the militant church as represented by the fighting faithful angels, who "In cubic phalanx firm advanced entire." The natural shape of fallen society is pyramidal, tending upward to a supreme earthly ruler. The church thus works in society as an emancipating and equalizing force: it transforms "ruling" in the sense of applying temporal force to "ruling" in Ezekiel's sense of measuring the temple of God. It accepts whatever temporal authority it finds in society, giving to Caesar what is Caesar's, and resisting Caesar only when he demands the things that are God's. When that happens, conscience is violated and the church may take up arms. The church does not, for Milton, transform society into anything that we should call a democracy, but it does work toward assimilating the people into the people of God, who are free because the gospel has made them free, and equal because God is no respecter of persons.

The freedom the gospel brings is a good but not a moral good: it is a more abundant life, and is not the opposite of evil so much as a greater power of fighting it. The next stage upward in man's evolution, or salvation as Milton would think of it, is the apocalypse, when the life represented by the gospel is finally separated from death. This ultimate separation is eloquently expressed in *Comus*, where the expression is all the more striking because *Comus* is not explicitly Christian in its symbolism:

> But evil on itself shall back recoil,
> And mix no more with goodness, when at last,
> Gathered like scum, and settled to itself,
> It shall be in eternal restless change
> Self-fed and self-consum'd. If this fail,
> The pillared firmament is rottenness,
> And earth's base built on stubble.

At this point man realizes that he has not been deprived of the tree of life after all, that it has been steadily growing inside him all through history, and that, when he separates himself from the communion with nature represented by the forbidden tree and attaches himself to the opposite communion, he will find himself, no less than the devils in hell, becoming what he has beheld.

The Garden
Within

ON THE TOP LEVEL OF THE ARTS we often meet a particular kind
of temperament that may be called the conservative temperament. Many great creators have become great primarily by
perfecting the forms they have inherited from their traditions.
They are usually artists who live entirely for their art, and have
little energy left over for any kind of personal expression that
is not absorbed into the art itself. When they experiment with
new forms and techniques, they normally do so as a means of
arriving at certain congenial conventions: they do not value
experiment for its own sake, but for the sake of the direction
it points out. They are deeply impersonal as a rule: we usually
know little about their lives that seems directly relevant to
what they produce, and their total body of work, from tenta-
tive beginning to disciplined end, reflects the organic evolution
of the forms they use. In English literature, Spenser seems to be
a poet of this conservative kind: he begins with experiment

but moves toward the single convention of the Spenserian stanza, and his work unfolds logically from the allegorical emblems contributed in his nonage to van der Noodt's *Theatre* to the great pageants of *The Faerie Queene*. Shakespeare, though always impossible to classify, has an obviously conservative strain in his temperament: nobody knows what his religious or political or social opinions were, and his personality seems so eerily self-effacing that he has irritated some people into a frenzy of trying to prove that he never existed.

There is a radical or revolutionary temperament, however, also found among the greatest creators, and which contrasts with the conservative one: the kind of contrast that is bound to impress us when we compare, say, Beethoven with Mozart or Bach, Michelangelo with Raphael, Victor Hugo with Flaubert, Turner with Constable, Byron or Shelley with Keats. To make such comparisons in detail might be of limited value and lead to considerable oversimplifying, but the contrast is there, a contrast between creative temperaments roughly parallel to the contrast of sublime and beautiful established by eighteenth-century critics in the arts themselves. It is clear that Milton belongs essentially to the radical group of artists, and many of his virtues and limitations become easier to understand when we keep this distinction in mind. If we do not keep it in mind, we may tend to sink into an unconscious preference for revolutionary or for conservative artists in general, and this may lead, as it has often led in the past, either to admiring Milton uncritically or disliking him uncritically.

The radical or revolutionary artist impresses us, first of all, as a tremendous personal force, a great man who happened to be an artist in one particular field but who would still have been a remarkable man whatever he had gone into. His art has in consequence a kind of oratorical relation to him: his creative *persona* reveals his personality instead of concealing it. He does not enter into the forms of his art like an indwelling spirit, but approaches them analytically and externally, tearing them to pieces and putting them together again in a way which expresses his genius and not theirs. In listening to the Kyrie of the Bach B minor Mass we feel what amazing things the fugue can do; in listening to the finale of Beethoven's Opus 106, we feel what amazing things can be done with the fugue. This latter is the feeling we have about *Comus* as a masque, for example, when we come to it from Jonson or Campion. Because the art of the revolutionary artist follows a rhythm of personal development external to itself, it goes through a series of metamorphoses: the revolutionary artist plunges into one "period" after another, marking his career off into separate divisions. The Beethoven of the last quartets is a different composer from the Beethoven of the earliest trios, and the Milton of *Paradise Regained* a different poet from the author of the Nativity Ode: but when we compare the Mozart of *The Magic Flute* with the infant prodigy of the 1760's we are more impressed by the continuity, and not only because Mozart died young.

The revolutionary aspect of Milton also comes out in that curious mania for doing everything himself which led him to produce his own treatise on theology, his own national history, his own dictionary and grammar, his own art of logic. In the only one of his published works that might conceivably be called an edition of somebody else, *The Judgment of Martin*

Bucer Concerning Divorce, he says impatiently that he is "a speaker of what God made mine own and not a translator." Both kinds of genius may seek for an art that transcends art, a poetry or music that goes beyond poetry or music. But the conservative artist finds—if this metaphor conveys anything intelligible to the reader—his greatest profundities at the centre of his art; the radical artist finds them on the frontier. Spenser develops toward the formal elaborations of Spenserian stanza and allegory; Bach toward the formal elaborations of the *Kunst der Fuge* and the *Musikalische Opfer*. Milton, like Beethoven, is continually exploring the boundaries of his art, getting more experimental and radical as he goes on, moving away from the complex stanza form of the Nativity Ode toward the free-verse recitatives of *Samson Agonistes*. And just as the work of the radical artist is iconoclastic in its attitude to tradition, so it is destructive in its effect on tradition. Gide's remark that the greatest French poet was "Victor Hugo, alas," is not, properly interpreted, a glib sneer but an accurate estimate of the place of such a poet in literary history. If there had been no Shakespeare, we should have to say "Milton, alas," to the parallel question about English poetry, and to the same question about Renaissance art there is no answer but "Michelangelo, alas."

The revolutionary artist does not have to be a social and political revolutionary as well, but he often is if he lives in a revolutionary time, though he is usually more of a nuisance than an asset to the causes he espouses. Every social revolution has the problem of establishing continuity with what it over-turns, continuity of authority, of administration, of habits of life. For the revolutionary artist, it is precisely the continuity in tradition that he rejects in his art, and hence he tends to see his political situations also vertically, as a break with continuity. Since Burke, we have become familiar with the conception of the continuum of dead, living and unborn as the one unbreakable social contract, as something that will go on no matter how great the changes in society. In Burke this is a conservative and anti-revolutionary theory, and his heavy emphasis on precedent, custom, prudence, even prejudice, and on the gradualness of all well-founded reform, belongs in that context. But the sense of a tradition of liberty, of social conflicts working toward a legal settlement with guarantees for both parties, of society modifying and adjusting its structure instead of attempting a new creation: this is a liberalizing sense for most of us, and the kernel of reality in the theory of progress.

In Milton's prose the lack of this sense of continuity, or more accurately the rejection of the values that go with it, is obvious and striking. In the Preface to *The Doctrine and Discipline of Divorce* Milton associates custom with error, and the association is habitual in his mind. *The Tenure of Kings and Magistrates* is a work of astonishing originality in its attempt to give some connected and coherent account of revolution as a force in history. But such an account demands documentation: documentation, in a work justifying a revolution, amounts to an appeal to precedent, and Milton will appeal to precedent only with the greatest reluctance:

But because it is the vulgar folly of men to desert their own reason, and shutting their eyes, to think they see best with other men's, I shall show, by such examples as ought to have most weight with us, what hath been done in this case heretofore.

Even in Milton's day there were books on how to win friends and influence people, but Milton was clearly not a student of them. Milton does not, however, think that arguments based on precedent and custom are good only for reassuring fools, otherwise he could hardly embark on them with such easy mastery as he does here and elsewhere. He feels rather that there is a greater and a lesser revolution to be achieved in his time. The greater one is religious, and is of apocalyptic proportions; the lesser one is political, and all arguments about custom and precedent and gradualness belong to it. If Milton thinks that the people of England are in danger of losing their sense of religious strategy by being confused about their political tactics, he can be very specific in discussing the latter, but he always sees them as contained within a larger context to which no short-run counsels of prudence apply. "In state," Milton remarks in *The Reason of Church Government*, "many things at first are crude and hard to digest, which only time and deliberation can supple and concoct. But in religion, where is no immaturity, nothing out of season, it goes far otherwise."

We spoke in the previous chapter of Milton's conception of liberty as the condition in which genuine action is possible: the condition, therefore, in which man acts as an instrument of the will of God. The state of liberty is attainable only by good men; it entails responsibility and rigorous discipline; it confers authority; it is always in accord with nature and with reason; it is the sole source of human dignity. The New Testament presents God as determined to set man free despite man's efforts to resist his own liberty, and this element in Christianity shows its contrast with all other religions: with, for example, the Homeric religion, which tells us that only the gods are free.

In Milton's day, the word liberty was also used in a technical and restricted sense as meaning spontaneity in the worship of God, particularly in a church service. Thus Richard Baxter says he once thought that a set form of liturgy had "nothing which should make the use of it, in the ordinary public worship, to be unlawful to them that have not liberty to do better." In most Nonconformist conceptions of worship, it is the Word of God that is recreated rather than his substantial presence, and hence the decisive event of the service of worship tends to be the sermon rather than the Eucharist, the substantial change in the elements of the Eucharist being denied. The preacher is not, in theory, ambitious to speak for himself, but only in the name of God, as the original prophets did, hence he tries to follow the gospel precepts about avoiding vain repetitions and being over-anxious about his own personal impact, and hopes to reach an utterance which will seem spontaneous to him and his hearers and yet will be guided by the Spirit he invokes. However narrow such a conception of Christian liberty may seem to us, it is the core of Milton's conception of it, and he is careful to ascribe a similar kind of spontaneity to the worship of Adam and Eve before their fall.

Of course a Protestant who also happens to be a major poet and a great prose writer as well cannot confine this conception of prophetic liberty of utterance to the pulpit: it spills over into the marketplace, into Parliament, and into literature, as *Areopagitica* shows. But the fact that liberty for Milton is always essentially verbal liberty, the power to know and utter, means that liberty for him has a specific focus which is not strictly that of either thought or action. We are all familiar with the famous phrase "reason is but choosing" in *Areopagitica*, which Milton himself thought so well of that he makes God the Father repeat it in *Paradise Lost* ("reason also is choice"). To choose means to act in the light of a certain vision of action, and reason in this sense is practical, as distinct from merely speculative, reason. I say merely speculative, because Milton has a low opinion of the kind of reason that finds no outlet in action: this is the reason Belial has, with his "thoughts that wander through eternity." Liberty for Milton is a release of energy through revelation, just as, to use the example of the previous chapter, we can set free our musical energies only through the study of music. There is a parallel distinction between rational action and action which has no vision to guide it. The latter is mindless, habitual, mechanical action, the action based on tradition, precedent, custom, the doing of what has been done before because it has been done before.

It follows that everything Milton associates with liberty is discontinuous with ordinary life. When he says in *Areopagitica* "there be delights, there be recreations and jolly pastimes, that will fetch the day about from sun to sun, and rock the tedious year as in a delightful dream," he is not objecting to pastime, but pointing out the delusory nature of the happiness that merely rides on nature's cyclical roller-coaster. The source of liberty is revelation: why liberty is good for man and why God wants him to have it cannot be understood apart from Christianity. Its product is reason, and reason of course is not confined to Christianity. But the effect of both revelation and reason is to arrest the current of mechanical habit. Revelation is a dialectical view of reality: it sees God as confronting the world, in the present moment, in an apocalyptic contrast of good and evil, life and death, freedom and bondage. Reason is less drastic, but its perspective is also dialectical and vertical. The consciousness withdraws from action and asks: is what we have been doing, without thinking about it, really worth doing? What would happen if we stopped doing it?

In this conception of reason as the withdrawing of consciousness from mechanical habit there is no sharp boundary line between it and what we should now call the imagination, nor between it and what we should call common sense, the inductive or empirical observation of what is really there. But there is the sharpest possible distinction between what Milton means by reason and what we should now mean by rationalization, the attempt to enlist reason in the service of passion. Rationalizing is always labyrinthine, like the attempts of the devils to work out a theology to justify their own revolt, which "found no end, in wandering mazes lost," or the arguments of Satan in the serpent, whose symbolic wrigglings "made intricate seem straight." What revelation sees is grace: what reason sees is nature, and both of these are simplifying visions, visions of order and coherence.

Rationalizing always leads back to the same major premise: it is good to go on doing what we are accustomed to do. It is not the reason that Milton identifies with choice, but the perverted reason that is designed to prevent us from making a choice and continue the perpetual-motion machine of unthinking action. Reason can only halt unthinking action when it presents a genuinely new vision. And where are we to obtain such a vision? Not from the nature outside us, because, as we saw in discussing Milton's conception of idolatry, the fall of man was the fall of Narcissus, and what we see in nature is like ourselves. It can only come from something inside us which is also totally different from us. That something is ultimately revelation, and the kernel of revelation is Paradise, the feeling that man's home is not in this world, but in another world (though occupying the same time and space) that makes more human sense. But such revelation has to be a personal force as well as a vision, for reason may see a better course of action without giving one the power to embark on it. And if genuine wisdom does not come from what is outside us in space, neither can it come from time, from experience or history or the knowledge of precedents and traditions that in our day inspire liberals and conservatives alike.

It follows that what man can do to achieve his own salvation, or even to achieve the social goals of reason and revelation, is largely negative. More precisely, it is, once more, iconoclastic. Man can demonstrate his willingness to be set free by knocking down his idols, but if he takes no advantage of the help then offered him, he will simply have to set new idols up, except that they will of course be the same old ones, error and custom. The prototype of all such efforts is that of Samson, who pulled down the Philistine temple and allowed the Israelite slaves to escape, but did not, by this act, save or redeem Israel. In his political attitude, it is somewhat disconcerting to realize that for Milton the most important symbol of the civil wars of his time was simply King Charles's head. The monarchy had become the English people's golden calf, and until it was pulled down, and the consequences of pulling it down faced, nothing else could be done.

We have spoken of the similarity of the structure of the first three books of *Paradise Lost* to that of the Jonsonian masque, a murky disorganized antimasque being followed by a vision of splendour and glory. But the Jonsonian masque normally leads to compliments and praises of the person in whose honour the masque is being held, and that person never speaks himself: if he did the spell would be broken and the masque would vanish into its elements, an illusion of tinsel and candlelight. In Milton, God the Father, in flagrant defiance of Milton's own theology, which tells us that we can know nothing about the Father except through the human incarnation of the Son, does speak, and with disastrous consequences. The rest of the poem hardly recovers from his speech, and there are few difficulties in the appreciation of *Paradise Lost* that are not directly connected with it. Further, he keeps on speaking at intervals, and whenever he opens his ambrosial mouth the sensitive reader shudders. Nowhere else in Milton is the contrast between the conceptual and the dramatic aspects of a situation, already glanced at, so grotesque: between recognizing that God is the source of all goodness and introducing God as a character saying: "I am the source of all goodness." The Father observes the improved behaviour of Adam after the fall and parenthetically remarks: "my motions in him." Theologically, nothing could be more correct: dramatically, nothing is better calculated to give the impression of a smirking hypocrite.

The speech the Father makes in Book Three has perhaps been modelled on the speech of Zeus at the opening of the *Odyssey*. But that speech is in perfect dramatic propriety. Zeus is merely saying that men often blame the gods for disasters they bring upon themselves, and gives an example, the death of Aegisthus, which has already occurred. What God does in Milton is to embark on a profoundly unconvincing argument purporting to show that Adam is responsible for his own fall, although God, being omniscient, foreknew it. But if God had foreknowledge he must have known in the instant of creating Adam that he was creating a being who would fall. And even if the argument held together, the *qui s'excuse s'accuse* tone in which it is delivered would still make it emotionally unconvincing.

Nor are the Father's other words and actions any more reassuring. They often do not seem very sharply distinguished from those of Satan. He professes a great concern for his creation ("thou knowest how dear to me are all my works," he says to the Son), yet when the news is brought him that one-third of his angelic creation has revolted against him he merely smiles. And although the Son is a considerably more attractive figure than the Father, he too has caught the contagion of unconcern: he is a "gracious Judge without revile," but there is nothing in him of Blake's Holy Word—

> Calling the lapsed Soul,
> And weeping in the evening dew

—weeping such tears as even Satan has the grace to shed for his woebegone followers. Satan interprets his one-third as nearly half, and God the Father speaks of his two-thirds as "far the greater part," but there is little moral difference between the two communiqués. Satan is never shown sending his followers on pointless errands, though the Father, according to Raphael, frequently does so.

We understand Milton very well when he shows us Satan accommodating himself to his actions with "Necessity, the tyrant's plea," but the Father seems equally caught in the trap of his own pseudo-logic:

> I else must change
> Their nature, and revoke the high decree
> Unchangeable, eternal.

We understand very well also the fact that Satan, in the council in hell, volunteers to journey to the earth a split second too quickly, because he will have to go anyway and there is no point in letting a minor devil get the credit for volunteering. The insidious corruption of power could hardly have found a better image. But it is difficult to see why the Father should be teasing the angels for a volunteer, considering that they have just proved their courage by an entirely unnecessary display of it. It seems, to sum this up, very strange that the main "argument," in the more limited sense of the doctrinal coherence of the poem, should be so largely entrusted to the one character who is conspicuously no good at argument; and I find that the objections of students and many critics to the poem usually reduce themselves to a single one: Why is everything rational in *Paradise Lost* so profoundly unreasonable?

I am concerned with the twentieth-century reader, and for him there is no answer in what may be called the Great Historical Bromide: the assertion that such problems would not exist for the seventeenth-century reader, who could not possibly have felt such resentment against a character clearly labelled "God," and talking like a seventeenth-century clergyman. Even so, some of these questions can be answered at once if we adopt the view, mentioned earlier, that the angels are undergoing a spiritual education as well as Adam. The sentry-duty that Raphael and others are assigned, "to inure our prompt obedience," may be only a military metaphor for such education. Similarly with the calling for volunteers: it is not lack of courage but lack of understanding that holds the angels back—for one thing, they do not know how to die. The dramatizing of the Atonement is a greater mystery than anything they have encountered before, and is necessary if they are to watch the working out of that drama with any comprehension. But still two questions keep revolving around Milton's portrayal of the Father. First, why is he there, in defiance of all poetic tact? Second, what has happened to the great Promethean rebel who steered his way through four revolutions and then, in his crowning masterpiece, associates rebellion with Satan and goodness and virtue with this grinning reactionary mask? I shall try to answer these questions separately, and then see if I can combine the answers in a way that may give us some useful insight into the poem.

First, then, the fact that the Father in Book Three claims foreknowledge but disclaims foreordination is to be related to our earlier principle that liberty, for Milton, arrests the current of habit and of the cause-effect mechanism. We are not to read the great cycle of events in *Paradise Lost* cyclically: if we do we shall be reading it fatalistically. For inscrutable reasons the Father begets the Son; that inevitably causes the jealousy and revolt of Satan; that inevitably causes Satan's defeat and expulsion; that inevitably causes his attempt to assault the virtue of Adam and Eve, and so on through the whole dreary sequence. If we think of human life in time as a horizontal line, the Father is telling us that he is not to be found at the beginning of that line, as a First Cause from which everything inevitably proceeds. He is above the line, travelling along with human life like the moon on a journey. The great events in *Paradise Lost* should be read rather as a discontinuous series of crises, in each of which there is an opportunity to break the whole chain. We see these crises forming when Satan argues himself out of the possibility of submission to God, and when Adam (with the aid of some arm-twisting on the part of the poet) absolves God from any responsibility for his own sin.

The failures, like the two great falls, look inevitable because they are failures, but the crucial victory, Christ's victory recorded in *Paradise Regained*, is not inevitable at all, at least from any point of view that we can take. At each crisis of life the important factor is not the consequences of previous actions, but the confrontation, across a vast apocalyptic gulf, with the source of deliverance. So whatever one thinks of the Father's argument, some argument separating present knowledge and past causation is essential to Milton's conception of the poem.

It seems to me—I have no evidence that this is Milton's view—that what God is saying in *Paradise Lost* is similar in many respects to what God is saying in the Book of Job. After the dialogue with the three friends and Elihu has reached a deadlock, God enters the argument himself with a series of rhetorical questions asking Job if he knows as much as God does about the creation. He seems to be trying to bully Job into submission by convicting him of ignorance of the divine ways. But perhaps his meaning can be taken differently. Perhaps he is merely discouraging Job from looking horizontally along a cause-effect sequence until he reaches a First Cause at the creation. Job is not even given the explanation that has been given the reader in the story of Satan's wager. It is not how he got into his calamity but how he can get out of it that is important, and this latter involves a direct and vertical relation between God and Job in the present tense.

There remains the question of what has happened to the political revolutionary in *Paradise Lost*. When he first seriously considered possible epic subjects, around the later 1630's, Milton tells us, he thought of Arthur as his hero. It is interesting to speculate about what Milton might have done with Arthur, as compared, say, with his two great predecessors Malory and Spenser. In Malory there is a graded series of knights, each knight being better than any other knight he can knock off his horse. Lancelot by this standard is the best knight in the world, "but if it were Sir Tristram"; the pagan knight Palomides is third, and Gawain and Gareth follow. Arthur, though an able knight and treated with respect as king, is by no means at the top of this list of seeded players, and if he goes into a tournament disguised and comes up against Lancelot or Tristram, down he goes over his horse's crupper. Malory reflects the society of the fifteenth-century baronial wars, where the king, though he may struggle into ascendancy for a time, may well be less permanently powerful than a great noble like the Earl of Warwick. In Spenser, Arthur is qualitatively different in strength and courage from all the knights of the Faerie Queene's court, who are related to him somewhat as the apostles are to Christ—the analogy is strained, but, considering the allegory, not pointless. Spenser is reflecting the mystique of the Tudor monarchy, and the skill with which its propaganda transformed a bastard Welsh ancestry into a myth of a reborn British Messiah. The Round Table, symbol of a feudal king's role as merely *primus inter pares*, is of no use to Spenser. But how could Arthur have been made, as he surely would have been made had Milton written an Arthurian epic before 1645, a symbol of the reformed church and Parliament triumphant over the encroachments of the king? For Arthur is a king, or prince, and any symbolism attached to him would have to reflect the fact.

Such a poem would have to make an extensive use of myth, and be closer in technique to *Comus* than to *Paradise Lost*. The more we think of Arthur historically, the more he tends to vanish into a period much like that of Milton's own time as Milton eventually came to conceive it, when the Britons, after throwing off the tyranny of Rome, collapsed under the tyranny of the English. There is not much left of Arthur in the *History of Britain*, and the place he might have had is occupied by a gloomy "digression" on how a nation may be led to rid itself of its masters and still not be capable of a rational freedom, in Gibbon's phrase. In *The Reason of Church Government* Milton speaks of looking for a hero "before the Conquest," restricting himself to that period for many reasons, one of which may have been that the Crusades began immediately afterwards, and he wanted neither competition nor association with Tasso's theme.

Of this mythical Arthur we have only a tantalizing allusion in *Mansus* to an Arthur making wars beneath the earth ("Arturumque etiam sub terris bella moventem"), indicating that Milton may have been thinking of Arthur as a figure like Blake's Orc, a revolutionary power hidden among the people, regarded as evil by his enemies, yet able to emerge and break the Saxon phalanxes in war. We also have that amazing poem *De Idea Platonica quemadmodum Aristoteles intellexit*, a poem in which the unborn embryos of Blake's Albion, Shelley's Prometheus and Dylan Thomas' "long world's gentleman" can be seen faintly stirring, where we meet an "archetypal giant" (*archetypus gigas*) who is not Adam but an eternal and incorruptible image of man, at once single and universal (*unusque et universus*). To these we may add the remark in *Of Reformation*, the earliest of the anti-Episcopal pamphlets: "A Commonwealth ought to be but as one huge Christian personage, one mighty growth, and stature of an honest man." These vague hints of a subterranean warrior and of a single human body who is both social and individual in form are not enough to base any theory on: they merely indicate the kind of imagery that might have attached itself to a revolutionary hero at this period of Milton's development.

The conception of society in *Paradise Lost* is quite as revolutionary as it is in the earlier prose. When Milton says of the Star Chamber that it has now "fallen from the stars with Lucifer," or that "Lucifer before Adam was the first prelate angel," he is suggesting what the opening books of *Paradise Lost* make clear: that hell is the model for perverted orders of society, whether in state or church. There can be no objection to monarchy as such, for Milton, only to monarchy as a possible focus for idolatry, but the tendency for a king to acquire the same kind of "false glitter" that Satan still has in hell is endemic in monarchy. The temporal authority represented by Nimrod in Book Twelve derives its structure from the demonic warrior aristocracy, and this authority, however inevitable, is still a usurpation:

> And from Rebellion shall derive his name,
> Though of Rebellion others he accuse.

What is harder to understand is, first, why the imagery of dictatorial power is attached to heaven as well as hell, and, second, what has happened to the conception of a revolutionary hero.

There is such a figure in Milton, but we have to look for it in his Samson rather than in his Satan. Samson in the Book of Judges is a typical boaster or trickster hero, whose strength reminds us of Hercules, but who never does anything good-natured or unselfish, as Hercules often does. He is given rather to practical jokes in extremely doubtful taste, such as setting fire to the tails of foxes and turning them into the fields of Philistine farmers to burn up their crops. Milton's skill in transforming this overgrown juvenile delinquent into a figure of such dignity and power is extraordinary, but even so there could hardly be a greater contrast between his shaggy ferocity and the demure suburban gravity of Adam. Adam is what leaders of men were intended to be, peaceful patriarchs; Samson is what the ascendancy of Nimrod and the later Philistines has forced human leaders to become. The difference in context is emphasized by the role of the heroine. We saw that Eve is human, not demonic, although permanently entrapped by something demonic after her fall, just as Cleopatra is permanently entrapped by Egypt. Delilah, however, is purely a tentacle of a Philistine society, and as such perhaps the nearest thing to a real siren in all English drama: a dry, crepitating, whispering evil, audible and tangible but not visible, full of the unbearable pathos of the cast off and forsaken, able, like Dido in hell, to unsettle her former lover's self-respect, yet never quite becoming human.

From the Philistine point of view it is Samson who is the sinister and demonic figure, an "evening dragon" descending on the roosts of the "villatic fowl." We saw earlier that in Milton's view the church should accept whatever temporal authority is provided for it, but that if the Christian conscience is violated the church may become a revolutionary force. Samson's life in Gaza is similarly based on a rigid separation of spiritual from temporal authority: as soon as his religious integrity is touched by his having to appear in the temple of Dagon, that is the end of the temple of Dagon. But his tragedy is similar in many respects to the tragedy of Coriolanus in Shakespeare. Like Coriolanus, "his heart's his mouth": he has nothing of the astuteness or the sense of obstacles that a leader must have if he is to crystallize a society around his leadership. Samson, as a leader, can only smash Philistines with his own hands: he cannot build an Israelite society, and is so loosely attached to his own people that he takes no responsibility for the fact that "Israel still serves with all his sons." True, the chorus of Danites, standing around uttering timid complacencies in teeth-loosening doggerel, are not a very reassuring social object; but they are what they are largely because Samson is no David. In his battles and final martyrdom Samson is an Old Testament prototype of Christ, but the aspect of the Messiah he typifies is the terrible blood-soaked figure of Isaiah who has trodden the winepress alone.

I have not spoken of the individual aspect of Milton's Samson because I am not concerned here with *Samson Agonistes* as such, only with Milton's view of the nature and function of the revolutionary hero in a revolutionary situation. Milton naturally had a good deal of respect for the political wisdom that dwells with prudence, that tacks and veers and catches the wind and makes the best of the confused mixture of good and evil which is human life. In the notebook in which he considers subjects for epic and tragedy, he does not mention Arthur, but he does pause at the name of Alfred the Great, "whose actions are well like those of Ulysses." He is willing to consider Oliver Cromwell as an emergency leader, like the judges of Israel to whom Samson belonged, but is at pains to point out that peace is not merely the end of a war, but a qualitatively different human condition from war, and one that requires far more complex qualities than the army commander as such possesses.

In a Catholic poet—Dante is the obvious example—the separation of divine and demonic worlds would be something that man sees or participates in through a process of sacramental discipline, which continues in the next world in the form of purgatory. But for Milton such revelation cannot come from anything continuous, however important habit and discipline may be in themselves. The place of sacrament and purgatory in his work is taken by the temptation, the agon or contest which is the theme of all four of his major poems. Each of these crises presents continuous and habitual life with an interruption, in which reality is split vertically into two opposed orders. The Lady in *Comus*, Christ in *Paradise Regained*, and Samson in *Samson Agonistes*, all adhere steadily to the divine vision, and as they do so the demonic world becomes more and more obviously demonic. But the victory over temptation leads to an exhaustion of power, and in the moment of victory power flows in from a source that is both identical with and different from the victor. Sabrina restores to the Lady her own power of movement; Christ is sustained on the pinnacle of the temple by the Father whose "Godhead" he carries; Samson changes his mind about going to the temple of Dagon in a way that shows that his mind has been changed for him.

The theme of the externalizing of the demonic and the internalizing of the divine runs through every aspect of Milton's writing. We have seen how the law is a tyranny to a criminal, for whom it is external, and how it is irksome and frustrating to us as long as we think of it as command rather than condition. The Word of God is a collection of dark sayings and hard names as long as it is a book in front of us, but swallowed by us, so to speak, as Ezekiel swallowed his roll, it becomes the charter of human dignity. We see this process of going from the book to the internal scripture dramatized in the summary of the Bible that Michael gives to Adam, which begins as a series of visions and then, after Abraham's act of faith in leaving Chaldea, is simply narrated. Milton appears to mean by the Holy Spirit what God gives to his creatures, which may be anything from life itself to a specific talent for writing poetry. It is this Spirit that understands the Bible, and that acts as the "umpire conscience" in the mind. The degeneracy of language, which has reduced "charity" to patronizing the indigent, has also reduced "conscience" to a subjective hunch derived from an infantile dependence on parents, which is not quite what Milton means by conscience. What he does mean is rather the power of living a free life. The Holy Spirit, which makes this possible, comes from God, and therefore tries to return to him, bringing us along in the process. But because it is the God within, it is where all liberty starts.

In *Paradise Lost*, of course, it is Paradise itself that is internalized, transformed from an outward place to an inner state of mind. We saw that Eden is finally washed away in the flood, in order to show that for God there is no longer anything sacred which can be located in either outward space or in past time. The world we fell from we can return to only by attaining the kind of freedom to which all education, as Milton defines it, leads, and it is this freedom that is said by Michael to be a happier paradise than that of the original garden.

Applying this principle of internalizing and spiritual discernment to the reading of *Paradise Lost* itself, we find in that poem a father-figure who seems harsh, arbitrary, inscrutable, and more given to rationalization than to reason. There is nothing to be done with this objectionable creature except swallow him. The heaven of *Paradise Lost*, with God the supreme sovereign and the angels in a state of unquestioning obedience to his will, can only be set up on earth inside the individual's mind. The free man's mind is a dictatorship of reason obeyed by the will without argument: we go wrong only when we take these conceptions of kingship and service of freedom as *social* models. Absolute monarchs and their flunkeys on earth always follow the model of hell, not of heaven. The cleavage between the conceptual and the dramatic aspects of the Father clears up when we realize that the one is the opposite of the other. The reason why kingship on earth is so apt to become idolatrous is precisely that it is the external projection of the inner sovereignty of God. This projection will eventually disappear even in heaven itself, as God tells us:

> For regal sceptre then no more shall need;
> God shall be all in all.

God's sovereignty, therefore, has its earthly model in the mind of the Enoch or Noah or Samson who refuses to compromise with evil, refuses to admit any of the arguments that evil advances in favour of compromise, and who, faced with the supreme test, can produce out of some unknown depth the power to suffer and die. This power suffers alone: Christ renounced the help of legions of angels when captured in the garden, just as he went out alone to win the war in heaven after the legions of angels had done their best, and just as Adam is told by Raphael that, whether there are other beings in other worlds or not, he must, like Beowulf, fight his dragon alone. Something of this lonely fight comes into Milton's personal statements in *Paradise Lost*: the cold climate, the late age, blindness, the loss of touch with literary fashions evidenced in the old-style blank verse, the religious and therefore conventionally unheroic subject, all suggest a kind of last-ditch desperateness. The lonely fight in the life of Christ is the theme of *Paradise Regained*, the subject of our last chapter.

We seem to find in Milton, then, a revolutionary who became disillusioned with the failure of the English people to achieve a free commonwealth, and was finally compelled to find the true revolution within the individual. Reactionaries and obscurantists of all kinds are always delighted with this solution, because they know of no conception of the individual except the opaque ego and Satan's defiant "here at least we shall be free," in a world far removed from any threat to the status quo. Of course it is true that Milton turned from social to individual and poetic activity after 1660: the personal reasons are obvious enough, but it is hard to think of *Paradise Lost* as some kind of consolation prize. An original purchaser, standing at a bookstall with the surge and thunder of the mighty poem breaking over him, might well have asked: "But this is a blind, defeated, disillusioned, gouty old man: where did he get all this energy?" It is a fair question, even if it may not have an answer.

We have got far enough with *Paradise Lost* to see that we have to turn its universe inside out, with God sitting within the human soul at the centre and Satan on a remote periphery plotting against our freedom. From this perspective, perhaps, we can see what Blake meant when he said that Milton was a true poet and of the devil's (i.e., the revolutionary) party without knowing it. The more we study the poem, the more doubtful we become of the last three words, yet they do say something that is true. In dealing with Satan, Milton moves with superb confidence, because Satan is his poetic creature: he knows what he means by Satan and he knows how to realize a Satanic personality. The weak spots of the poem, such as God's speech in Book Three and Raphael's doubtful answer to Adam in Book Eight, are not so well realized poetically, because what Milton wants the reader to grasp is something existential, something beyond poetry. The better we know the poem, the more important become these passages that we cannot fully understand without possessing the poem.

All revolutionary myths are sleeping-beauty myths: what the revolution attacks is a usurpation, and what it replaces it with is historically, or at least morally, prior to the usurpation. The Protestant in Milton fought for the restoration of the primitive church of the gospels, against the usurpation of tradition, or custom and error. The humanist in him fought for the ancient liberty of the Greek and Roman republics against the usurpation of kings and priests. The Parliamentarian in him fought for the liberties of the lords and commons against the usurpations of Star Chamber and royal prerogative. All these are causes rooted in history, models of the past to be recreated in the future. There is no evidence that Milton ceased to believe in any of these causes, but he was driven by a deeper logic than that of disillusionment to study the primal pattern, the ultimate myth of the gate of origin, the definitive insight into how things came to be, which Raphael gives Adam as the essence of his message and which Satan cuts off from himself. Milton's source told him that although heaven is a city and a society, the pattern established for man on earth by God was not social but individual, and not a city but a garden.

The ultimate precedent, therefore, in which all other precedents are rooted, is not Utopian but Arcadian, not historical but pastoral, not a social construct but an individual state of mind. In the Old Testament, Moses, the law, comes to the border of the Promised Land which only Joshua, who has the same name as Jesus, can conquer. But in the Old Testament the Promised Land becomes the society of Israel, whereas in Milton, when Jesus defeats Satan in the desert, it is "Eden" that he raises in the wilderness, and his mission is not to restore any "earthly Canaan," but to bring back

> Through the world's wilderness long wandered Man
> Safe to eternal Paradise of rest.

Social and political revolution, to be of any use, has to be related to the vision of what it is to achieve. And we find that the goal of man's quest for liberty is individualization: there is no social model or ideal state in the human mind. Social relations are always in the sphere of the law. Even the church is a by-product of the individuals composing it who possess the higher or internal form of scripture in their minds: the church is not, beyond a certain point, the teacher of these individuals, but the product of their dialogue with one another. Milton divides the cause of liberty into civil, domestic and religious spheres, and he fought with courage and high intelligence for the civil and religious causes as he understood them. But it is domestic liberty that is really Milton's own sphere:

the cause of education and free speech, and a conception of marriage which finds its model in Adam and Eve alone in Eden. And while civil and religious liberty are the concern of skilful and subtle dialecticians, domestic liberty, the goal of human development itself, takes us from dialectic to the emblematic vision or parable, and requires a poet.

Many critics of Milton tell us that Milton's style is oppressively brocaded and ornate, a kind of Anglicized Latin, sonorous and lofty but never direct or simple. There are two groups of such critics, the ignorant and the perverse: one group is numerous and the other influential, and those whose notions of Milton were formed in youth by the first book of *Paradise Lost* have little power of resistance to them. It seems a curious view of a poet who distinguished poetic from discursive writing as more simple, sensuous and passionate. Simplicity of language is a deep moral principle to Milton: whenever he is attacking the tyranny of tradition it is always the humanist's contempt for the "knotty Africanisms" and gabbling abstractions of theological lawyers that is foremost in the attack. The complex historical issues and formidable titles of such works as *Tetrachordon*, *Eikonoklastes*, or *Animadversions upon the Remonstrant's Defence* often prevent us from discovering that they are brilliant polemical writings, crackling with wit and epigram and the free play of an exuberant and, granted the polemical context, good-humoured mind. Milton was, so far as I know, the first great English writer to fight for semantic sanity, to urge his readers not to react automatically to smear or bogey words like "heretic" or "blasphemer," but to look at such words and see what, if anything, they really mean. He can show amazing insight in defining the mythical complexes that organize the processes of confused and panic-stricken minds:

> So that we, who by God's special grace have shaken off the servitude of a great male tyrant, our pretended father the pope, should now, if we be not betimes aware of these wily teachers, sink under the slavery of a female notion, the cloudy conception of a demy-island mother.

In handling scriptural quotations, particularly in the divorce tracts, he is a precise and delicate stylist in his constant feeling for the context and decorum of the passages he deals with, and he is a stylist too in his contempt for the trumpery show of logic by which malice can always score a point over charity. He is never tired of defending vigorous and outspoken language—to such an extent, in fact, that it seems strange that there should be no passage needing such defence in the whole of his poetry, and few if any in his prose. He constantly dwells on the simplicity and plainness of the gospels, and his own poetic style, however erudite, is seldom ambiguous, even in the proper critical sense of that term. He employs ambiguity only for very special contexts, such as the word "fruit" in the first line of *Paradise Lost* and the word "solitary" in the last. Wherever we turn in Milton, we find his awareness of the fact that oratory and rhetoric cannot function properly unless they can achieve the kind of simplicity that means what it says, and that they cannot attain this simplicity unless they are employed in the service of human liberty. Hence a decline in style and literary sensitivity is one of the first signs of general decline:

> Therefore when the esteem of Science, and liberal study waxes low in the Commonwealth, we may presume that also there all civil Virtue, and worthy action is grown as low to a decline: and then Eloquence, as it were consorted in the same destiny, with the decrease and fall of virtue corrupts also and fades.

Or, even more explicitly:

While it is Plato's opinion that by a change in the manner and habit of dressing serious commotions and mutations are portended in a commonwealth, I, for my part, would rather believe that the fall of that city and its low and obscure condition were consequent on the general vitiation of its usage in the matter of speech.

Paradise Lost, in the final period of Milton's career, represents not only an intensification but a colossal simplifying of his thought and vision. The story of Adam, in his day, was, as poetic material, the dreariest commonplace: Milton reached it by cutting through all the complex religious and political issues of his day until he got down to the myth that generated them, the myth that creates in us, whether we always know it or not, the unshakable conviction that the real form of human life is a form of leisure and peace and freedom, the conviction that is both the light of intelligence and the heat of courage. Because he reached it the hard way, the story of Adam in Milton has the simplicity that is so like the commonplace, and yet so different, the simplicity that keeps us in the centre of human experience. As commonplace, the story of Adam is rationalized superstition, asserting that for mysterious reasons in a dim past man is forever prevented from getting anything he really wants. Reached the way Milton reached it, it becomes the counterpart in history to what the music of the spheres is in nature: a glimpse of a central point of order which absorbs both hope and disillusionment into serenity.

Revolt in the Desert

AMONG THE LEAST FULLY REALIZED PARTS OF *Paradise Lost* is what seems a hurried and perfunctory summary of the Bible in the latter part of Michael's revelation. The reason is that such events as the Incarnation and the Last Judgment cannot be given their full poetic resonance at that point in the *Paradise Lost* scheme, otherwise the conclusion would become top-heavy. They must either be dramatized separately or assumed to have their importance already understood by the reader. *Paradise Regained* dramatizes the third of four epiphanies in which Christ confronts Satan: it refers back to the original war in heaven as recounted in *Paradise Lost*, and forward to the final binding of Satan prophesied in the Book of Revelation. The defeat of Satan as tempter fulfils the prophecy in Genesis that the seed of Adam shall "bruise the serpent's head," which Satan refers to so light-heartedly in *Paradise Lost*.

This imagery suggests the romance theme of a knight-errant killing a dragon, and is one of several such images in the Bible. Besides the serpent in Eden, the Old Testament speaks of a dragon or sea monster, called "leviathan," or "Rahab," who was defeated once at the creation and is to be destroyed, or, in the metaphor of the sea serpent, hooked and landed, on the day of judgment. A comparison of Satan to the leviathan appears early in *Paradise Lost*. Isaiah refers both to the previous and to the future victories over this leviathan, and Ezekiel and Isaiah appear to identify him with Egypt as the symbolic land of bondage. In the Book of Revelation this figure becomes a dragon with seven heads and ten horns, whose tail draws a third of the stars from heaven, the basis of Milton's account of Satan's fall. The connection of this dragon with Egypt in Milton is indicated in Michael's references to the Nile's seven mouths and to the plagues of Egypt as the ten wounds of the river dragon. In the symbolism of Revelation, again, the Satan of Job and the gospels, the serpent of the Eden story, and the leviathan of the prophecies, are all explicitly identified.

From this is derived the conventional symbol of Christ as a dragon-killer, such as we have in medieval sculptures portraying him with a dragon or basilisk under his feet. In the first book of *The Faerie Queene*, the story of St. George and the dragon is used as an allegory of the imitation of Christ by the church. St. George's dragon in Spenser is identified with the Satan-serpent-leviathan complex in the Bible, and as a result of St. George's victory the parents of his lady Una, who are Adam and Eve, are restored to their inheritance, the Garden of Eden, which is also the unfallen world. In *The Reason of Church Government* Milton refers to the allegory of St. George and "the king's daughter, the Church." Michael explains to

Adam, however, that the contest of Christ and Satan will be not a physical but a spiritual and intellectual fight, the cutting weapons used being those of dialectic, and the true dragon being a spiritual enemy.

I mentioned earlier the passage in *The Reason of Church Government* in which Milton speaks of the literary genre of the "brief epic." As *Paradise Regained* is clearly Milton's essay in the brief epic, and as the model for that genre is stated by Milton to be the Book of Job, we should expect *Paradise Regained* to have a particularly close relation to that drama. In Job the contest of God and Satan takes the form of a wager on Job's virtue, and the scheme of *Paradise Regained* is not greatly different, with Christ occupying the place of Job. Satan, we notice, soon disappears from the action of Job, and when Job's mind is finally enlightened by God, God's speech consists very largely of discourses on two monsters, behemoth and leviathan, the latter of whom, the more important, is finally said to be "king over all the children of pride." These monsters seem to represent an order of nature over which Satan is permitted some control, but, in a larger perspective, they are seen to be creatures of God. By pointing these beasts out to Job, God has, so to speak, put them under Job's feet, and taken Job into his own protection. Thus the victory of Job is, in terms of this symbolism, a dialectical victory over both Satan and leviathan, Satan and leviathan being much the same thing from different points of view.

In more traditional views of the Incarnation the central point of the contest of Christ and Satan is located between Christ's death on the cross and his resurrection. It is then that he descends to hell, harrows hell, and achieves his final victory over hell and death. In medieval paintings of the harrowing of hell, hell is usually represented as leviathan, a huge open-mouthed monster into which, or whom, Christ descends, like the Jonah whom Christ accepted as a prototype of his own Passion. For Milton, however, the scriptural evidence for the descent into hell was weak, and besides, Milton believed that the whole of Christ's human nature died on the cross, with no soul or spirit able to survive and visit hell. In the synoptic gospels, the temptation immediately follows the baptism. Milton's view of baptism is an exception to his generally anti-sacramental attitude to biblical symbolism: he is willing to see in it a symbol of the three-day crisis of Christian redemption, death, burial and resurrection. So the temptation is what becomes for Milton the scripturally authorized version of the descent into hell, the passing into the domain of Satan, and the reconquest of everything in it that is redeemable. Certain features, such as the bewilderment of the forsaken disciples and the elegiac complaint of the Virgin Mary at the beginning of the second book, might seem more natural if Milton had followed medieval tradition in making *Paradise Regained* the harrowing of hell. In any case Christ's withdrawal from the world at this point is the opposite of a "fugitive and cloistered virtue," as he is being led directly into the jaws of hell itself, and not yet as a conqueror.

The Bible gives us two parallel versions of the fall and redemption of man. The first is the *Paradise Lost* version. Adam falls from the garden into a wilderness, losing the tree of life and the water of life. Christ, the second Adam, wins back the garden ("Eden raised in the waste wilderness") and restores to man the tree and river of life. This version is elaborated by

Spenser as well as Milton, for in Spenser the fight between St. George and the dragon takes place at the boundary of Eden, and St. George is refreshed by the paradisal well of life and tree of life, which continue in the church as the sacraments of baptism and communion. As the natural home of Christ on earth is a fertile garden, the Eden in which he walked in the cool of the day, so the natural home of devils is the wilderness, "A pathless desert dusk with horrid shades," a blasted land like the country traversed in the *City of Dreadful Night* or by Browning's Childe Roland, the sort of scene one instinctively calls "God-forsaken," where the panic inspired by hunger, lost direction and loneliness would have unsettled the reason of most people in much less than forty days.

Inside the story of Adam comes the second version, the story of Israel, who falls from the Promised Land into the bondage of Egypt and Babylon. Besides being a second Adam, Christ is a second Israel, who wins back, in a spiritual form, the Promised Land and its capital city of Jerusalem. In this capacity the story of the Exodus, or deliverance of Israel from Egypt, prefigures his life in the Gospels. Israel is led to Egypt through a Joseph; Christ is taken to Egypt by a Joseph. Christ is saved from a wicked king who orders a massacre of infants; Israel is saved from the slaughter of Egyptian first-born. Moses organizes Israel into twelve tribes and separates it from Egypt at the crossing of the Red Sea; Christ gathers twelve followers and is marked out as the Redeemer at his baptism in the Jordan, which the Israelites also later cross. Israel wanders forty years in the wilderness; Christ forty days. The Israelites receive the law from Mount Sinai; the gospel is preached in the Sermon on the Mount, which in its structure is largely a commentary on the Decalogue. The Israelites are plagued by serpents and are redeemed by placing a brazen serpent on a pole. This, like the story of Jonah, is also accepted as a prototype of the Crucifixion by Christ himself. The Israelites conquer the Promised Land under Joshua, who has the same name as Jesus, corresponding to Christ's victory over death and hell, as, in the church's calendar, Easter immediately follows the commemorating of the temptation in Lent. Thus when the Angel Gabriel tells the Virgin Mary to call her child's name Jesus, or Joshua, the meaning is that the reign of the law is now over and the assault on the Promised Land has begun.

The death of Moses just outside the Promised Land represents the inability of the law alone to redeem mankind, as Milton emphasizes both in *Paradise Lost* and in *The Christian Doctrine*. The difficulty of the temptation for Christ, as *Paradise Regained* presents it, is complicated by the fact that Christ is still, at this stage of his career, within the law. His temptation is part of a much subtler process of separating, in his own mind, the law which is to be annihilated from the law which is to be fulfilled and internalized. Milton explicitly says that Christ in the wilderness "into himself descended," and employed his time in clarifying his own mind about the nature of his Messianic mission. We see little of what is actually passing in Christ's mind, but as his refusal of one after another of Satan's temptations drives Satan on to display his resources in a steadily rising scale of comprehensiveness and intensity, the poetic effect is that of negatively clarifying Christ's own thoughts. The climax of the temptation corresponds to the death of Moses: it is the point at which Jesus passes from obedience to the law to works of faith, from the last Hebrew prophet to the founder of Christianity.

The typical Old Testament figures who represent the law and the prophets, respectively, are Moses and Elijah, who accompany Jesus in the Transfiguration and are the two "witnesses" to his teaching in the Book of Revelation. Both of them prefigured the forty-day retirement and fast of Jesus in their own lives. The Old Testament says that Elijah will come again before the Messiah, a prophecy fulfilled by John the Baptist, but in a sense Moses has to be reborn too, as the law is fulfilled in the gospel. The Bible suggests the possibility that Moses did not die but was, like Elijah, transported directly to Paradise. An early version of *Paradise Lost* was to have begun with some speculations on this point.

Christ has fasted for forty days, and, as Luke remarks with some restraint, "he afterward hungered." He has a Freudian wish-fulfilment dream, like Eve in *Paradise Lost*, in which memories of Old Testament stories of prophets are mingled with food. Still, he is not hungry until after the first temptation to turn stones to bread, which consequently has nothing to do with hunger but is superficially an appeal to his charity, corresponding to the miraculous provision of manna in the Exodus. Jesus' answer that man shall not live by bread alone is a quotation from a passage in Deuteronomy that refers to the giving of manna. A contrast is involved between the material bread of the law and the bread of life in the gospel. This contrast distinguishes the gospel from what, for Milton, was the sacramental fallacy, the tendency to translate the Jewish ceremonial code into Christian terms, the fallacy that produced the doctrine of transubstantiation, which Milton characterizes as a banquet of cannibals. Milton's interest in this first temptation, however, is less in the temptation as such than in the tactical manœuvre which Satan makes after his disguise is penetrated.

Milton's most obvious source for *Paradise Regained*, apart from the Bible itself, was Giles Fletcher's poem *Christ's Victory and Triumph*, of which the temptation forms an episode. In Fletcher, the first temptation is primarily a temptation of despair, and hence closely follows the episode of Despair in the first book of *The Faerie Queene*. Milton's Christ uses only the term "distrust," but still Milton is here the poetic grandson of Spenser. Despair's argument in Spenser is based on the logic of law without gospel, i.e., sin is inevitable, and the longer one lives the more one sins. The emotional overtones are those of the indolence and passivity which is at the heart of all passion, and some of them are echoed in the argument of Comus to the Lady:

> Refreshment after toil, ease after pain.

Satan's argument in *Paradise Regained* is a refinement of Despair's. Good and evil are inseparable in the fallen world, and, in a world where all instruments are corrupted, one must either use corrupt instruments or not act at all. The use of evil or Satanic means being inevitable, Satan himself must be a reluctant agent of the will of God, as long as we can preserve a belief in the will of God. In terms of the law alone, which can discover but not remove sin, this argument is more difficult to refute than it looks—in fact it could be a clever parody of the central argument of *Areopagitica*. Christ's answer, leading up as it does to a prophecy of the cessation of oracles and the coming of the Word of God to the human heart, is based on the gospel or spiritual view of scripture. Satan has never met this view before, and is sufficiently baffled to retire and consult with his colleagues before going further.

The conflict in *Paradise Regained* is ultimately a spiritual one, but the basis of the human spirit is the physical body, and the body is the battlefield of the spirit. Milton is clear that the soul is the form of the body, and that there are not two essences in man. Another allegorical poem between *The Faerie Queene* and *Paradise Regained*, *The Purple Island*, by Giles Fletcher's brother Phineas, begins with a detailed allegory of the physical body and then expands into a psychomachia, in which the principals are Christ and the Dragon. This allegory is based on the defence of the House of Alma in the second book of *The Faerie Queene*, which presents the quest of Guyon, the knight of temperance or continence, the physical integrity which is not so much virtue as the prerequisite of virtue. The crucial ordeals of Guyon are the temptation of money in the cave of Mammon, mentioned by Milton in a famous passage in *Areopagitica*, and the Bower of Bliss, where the tempting agent is female and the temptation itself primarily erotic. In Giles Fletcher's version of the temptation of Christ the final temptation is modelled on the Bower of Bliss. Satan's rejection of Belial's proposal to tempt Christ with women indicates Milton's deliberate departure from Fletcher's precedent. Milton had already dealt with such themes in *Comus*. *Comus*, which leads up to Sabrina's deliverance of the Lady by sprinkling her with water, an act with some analogies to baptism, presents, so to speak, the temptation of innocence, where the assault on sexual continence is naturally central. *Paradise Regained* follows baptism, and presents the temptation of experience.

The sequence of temptations, which now proceeds unbroken to the end of the poem, begins, then, with an attack on the physical basis of Jesus' humanity. There are two of these temptations—a banquet and an offer of money; neither is in the gospels, and it is clear that the temptations of "Beauty and money" in the second book of *The Faerie Queene* are mainly responsible for them. They take place in a pleasant grove, and one line is a vestigial survival of the Bower of Bliss, with its triumph of artifice over nature:

> Nature's own work it seemed (Nature taught Art).

Attacks on temperance could be resisted by any genuine prophet or saint, or even by a virtuous heathen. Satan is an imaginative Oriental bargainer, and one has the feeling that although of course he would like to gain Christ as cheaply as possible, he is reconciled to seeing these temptations fail. His strategy, as we shall see, is cumulative, and individual temptations are expendable. The temptations of food and money continue the argument of the first temptation, in that they urge the necessary use of doubtful means for good ends. Their rejection establishes the principle, which is also in Spenser, that the moral status of the instrument depends on the mental attitude toward it. If the initial attitude is one of passive dependence, the instrument will become an illusory end in itself. It is not immediately apparent, however, why Satan has so much higher an opinion of food than of women as a temptation, even granting that there is really only one temptation of food.

We should be careful not to take anything in Satan's reply to Belial, such as his remark that beauty stands "In the admiration only of weak minds," at its face value. Nothing that Satan says in the poem is as trustworthy as that. He is, of course, right in thinking that Christ cannot be tempted to sins which are foreign to his nature; he can be tempted only to be some form of Antichrist, some physical or material counterpart of himself. But he is right for the wrong reasons.

If we look back at our earlier discussion of lust and greed, we can see that the initial attacks on Jesus are based on greed, and that lust, in its primitive sexual form, is what is sacrificed in Satan's gambit. The reason is that Satan assumes Christ to be a hero of some kind, in view of what was said of him at the baptism. If he is designed to redeem Adam, he must be strong at Adam's weak point of susceptibility to "female charm." For Satan, heroic action means his own type of aggressive and destructive parody-heroism, which is a form of lust. His assumption that the Messiah's heroism will be in some way of this type, or can be easily diverted to it, is genuine, and he is consequently willing to give Jesus credit for a heroic contempt of "effeminate slackness," besides being unwilling to put him prematurely on his guard by presenting him with a relatively crude form of lust. Satan's own contempt for the kind of heroism that Christ seems to prefer is also genuine, and for anyone else this would be itself a major temptation, a form of shame. Faithful in Bunyan, for example, remarks that shame, in the sense of worldly contempt, was his worst enemy. Satan, the accuser of Israel, is what, since Milton's day, we have learned to call a Philistine. Both Satan and Christ divide the world into the material and the spiritual, but for Satan the material is real and the spiritual is imaginary, or, as he says, "allegoric." It is only from Christ's point of view that he is an Archimago or master of illusion: from ours he is consistently a realist.

Hence, just as Comus puns on the word "nature," so all the elements of the dialectical conflict are attached to a material context by Satan and to a spiritual one by Christ. By rejecting everything that Satan offers in Satan's sense, Christ gets it again in its true or spiritual form, just as Adam, if he had successfully resisted his temptation, would still have become as the gods (i.e., the true gods or angels), knowing good, and evil as the possible negation of good. In *The Christian Doctrine* Milton speaks of the virtue of urbanity and its opposing vice of obscenity, which, he says, consists of taking words in a double sense. In this context he means what we mean by the *double entendre*: still, Christ is the source of urbanity and Satan of obscenity, and something of the *double entendre*, the great words "the kingdom, the power and the glory" profaned to their worldly opposites, runs all through Satan's speeches. As in the previous conflict, Satan is "scoffing in ambiguous words."

The opening colloquy between Satan and Christ in the first book is already a clash of oracular powers. Satan's dialectical instrument is the evasive or quibbling oracle, which cheats its hearer, as it did Macbeth, by double meanings that would be bad jokes if their serious consequences did not make them obscene. Christ speaks throughout with the simplicity and plainness that, as we saw, Milton emphasizes so much in the gospels. The climax of *Paradise Regained*, when Satan falls from the pinnacle and Christ stands on it, is marked by two very carefully placed Classical allusions, almost the only mythological ones in the poem. One is to Hercules and Antaeus, of which more later; the other is to Oedipus and the Sphinx. Christ has not only overcome temptation, but, as the Word of God, he has solved the verbal riddle of human life, putting all the words which are properly attributes of God into their rightful context.

The temptations which follow are temptations to false heroic action, and fall into three parts: the temptation of Parthia, or false power; the temptation of Rome, or false justice; and the temptation of Athens, or false wisdom. One problem of interpretation is raised by Milton's curious proportioning of emphasis. The temptation of Parthia seems much the crudest of the three: it is not easy to think of Jesus as some kind of Genghis Khan. Yet it takes up the entire third book, while the other two are huddled with the third temptation into the fourth.

In Jesus' day, with the memory of the Maccabees still vivid, the question of armed rebellion against Roman power was very insistent; it was the course that most Jews expected the Messiah to take, and had already been in the mind of the youthful Christ:

> victorious deeds
> Flamed in my heart, heroic acts, one while
> To rescue Israel from the Roman yoke.

And, though even then Christ thought of putting down violence rather than of using violence, still Satan's arguments on this point are unanswerable: to defeat Roman power by arms requires princely virtues, and princely virtues, as Machiavelli demonstrated, are not moral virtues, far less spiritual ones: they are martial courage and cunning, both demonic gifts. What Satan unwittingly does for Christ in the temptations of Parthia and Rome is to dramatize the nature of that aspect of law that is to be annihilated by the gospel—law as a compelling external force in which spiritual authority is subject to and administered by temporal authority.

Satan is shrewd enough to throw in the suggestion that, by gaining the power of Parthia, Christ will be able to realize the patriotic dream of reuniting the lost ten tribes with the Jewish remnant. In rejecting this, Christ rejects also the legal conception of Israel as a chosen people and is ready to usher in the new Christian conception of Israel as the body of believers. But there seems also to be some personal reference, however indirect, to the great blighted hope of Milton's political life.

The final binding of Satan, the last phase of the total cycle, is prophesied in the Book of Revelation, where, in the twelfth chapter, we have again a wilderness, a symbolic female figure representing the church, and a threatening dragon beaten off by Michael, the angelic champion of Israel, in a repetition of the first encounter. Milton, like everyone else, took the Book of Revelation to be in part a prophecy of the troubles the church was to suffer after the apostolic period. In *The Reason of Church Government* he attacks the supporters of tradition because they do not understand that the Book of Revelation foretells an apostasy of the church and "the Church's flight into the wilderness." Several times in the prose pamphlets Milton refers to the rebellion against Charles I in terms of the Exodus from Egypt, and expresses a hope that England will be a new chosen people, chosen this time for the gospel instead of the law, the rescued apocalyptic church coming out of the wilderness with Michael into a new Promised Land. In this role the English nation would represent the returning lost tribes, a new Israel taking up the cross that the Jews had rejected. By the time he wrote *Paradise Regained*, the English had chosen, in the terrible phrase of *The Ready and Easy Way*, "a captain back for Egypt." Yet even Milton cannot allow Christ to dismiss the unfaithful tribes, who have lost their birthright rather than their home, without adding a few wistful cadences in another key, too gentle in tone to be a direct reply to Satan, and at most only overheard by him:

> Yet he at length, time to himself best known,
> Rememb'ring Abraham, by some wondrous call
> May bring them back, repentant and sincere,
> And at their passing cleave the Assyrian flood,
> As the Red Sea and Jordan once he cleft,
> When to the Promised Land their fathers passed;
> To his due time and providence I leave them.

The temptation of Parthia, to ally the Messiah with an anti-Roman power in order to overthrow Rome, had thus been a temptation of Milton as well as of Milton's Christ. It is clear from what we have said in the previous chapter that if Milton had written an epic around the time he wrote *The Reason of Church Government*, it would have been more closely affiliated to the epic-romance convention established by Boiardo, Ariosto, and Spenser, in which Arthur would have represented a crusader or Christian warrior and some heroine an aspect of "the king's daughter, the Church," like Spenser's Una. But the female figure over whom physical wars are fought is likely to be closer to the erotic conventions "inductive mainly to the sin of Eve," to courtly love, uxoriousness and lust. The rejected romance tradition appears in Milton's reference to "The fairest of her sex, Angelica," where we might expect the more familiar Helen of Troy or Guinevere. The shadowy and insubstantial landscape of Boiardo may be Milton's reason for choosing it rather than a more concretely historical theme.

In *Paradise Regained* Satan displays all his kingdom: consequently Christ must refuse all of it, including much that in other contexts he might handle fearlessly. Later in his career he shows no hesitation in providing miraculous food, sitting at table with sinners, or accepting money and other gifts. But he has not yet entered on his ministry: the teaching and healing Christ that we know, with his compassion and courtesy, his love of children, and his sense of humour, has no place in Satan's kingdom. The haughtiness and aloofness of Christ mean that, before Christ can work in the world, he must recognize and repudiate all worldliness. In *Paradise Regained* Christ is looking at the world as it is under the wrath, as the domain of Satan. Wrath is the reaction of goodness contemplating badness; it is disinterested and impersonal, and is the opposite of anger or irritation. If God is capable of wrath, he must be incapable of irritation. This is the real reason for the difficulty we stumbled over earlier, the Father's being such a monster of indifference to his creation in *Paradise Lost* that he merely smiles when he observes that a third of his angels have revolted. The word "unmoved," so often applied to Christ in *Paradise Regained*, refers to his emotions as well as his intellect: Satan is condemned but not railed at. Christ cannot exercise mercy until he has separated it from sentimentality, and his comments on the misery of man under wrath are part of this separation. This means that once more we are faced with a contrast between the dramatic and the conceptual aspects of the situation. Dramatically, Christ becomes an increasingly unsympathetic figure, a pusillanimous quietist in the temptation of Parthia, an inhuman snob in the temptation of Rome, a peevish obscurantist in the temptation of Athens.

We said that when Adam decides to die with Eve rather than live without her, we are expected to feel some sympathy for Adam, to the point at least of feeling that we might well have done the same thing in his place, as, of course, we would. Conversely, one may almost say that the point at which the reader loses sympathy with Jesus in *Paradise Regained* is the point at which he himself would have collapsed under the temptation. All of us are, like Christ, in the world, and, unlike him, partly of it. Whatever in us is of the world is bound to condemn Christ's rejection of the world at some point or other. This aspect of the temptation story is the theme of the other great literary treatment of it, the Grand Inquisitor episode in *The Brothers Karamazov*, but it is present in Milton too.

Paradise Regained thus illustrates to the full the contrast between the dramatic and conceptual aspects of a situation that we have seen to be characteristic of Milton's temptation scenes. One might think that Milton had selected the temptation of Christ because it is, with the possible exception of the agony in the garden (on which Milton also meditated a "Christus patiens"), the only episode in which suspense and the feeling of the possible awful consequences of failure are consistently present. Christ's immediate discerning of Satan under his initial disguise, and his ability to reply "Why art *thou* solicitous?"

to every temptation, destroy all opportunity for narrative suspense. Of course Christ, like Adam, must be "sufficient to have stood, though free to fall," and he can hardly be sufficient to have stood if, like Eve, he can be deceived by a disguise, or if, like Uriel, he is too simple to understand hypocrisy. In any case dramatic propriety is on the side of clear vision: the more objective one is, the more easily one may see the subjective motivations in others, and anyone with Christ's purity of motivation would know the thoughts of others, as in the gospels he is said to do. Narrative suspense and dramatic sympathy go together: we can have them in *Samson Agonistes*, but they must be renounced here.

The reader may feel that the effect is to make both Christ and Satan seem bored with their roles, and that such boredom is infectious. Of course in long poems there are two areas of criticism, the structure or design and the poetic realization of details, and value-judgments established in one area are not transferable to the other. It is quite possible for a poem to be, as *Paradise Regained* may be, a magnificent success in its structure and yet often tired and perfunctory in its execution. In structure, however, *Paradise Regained* is not only a success but a technical experiment that is practically *sui generis*. None of the ordinary literary categories apply to it; its poetic predecessors are nothing like it and it has left no descendants. If it is a "brief epic," it has little resemblance to the epyllion; its closest affinities are with the debate and with the dialectical colloquy of Plato and Boethius, to which most of the Book of Job also belongs. But these forms usually either incorporate one argument into another dialectically or build up two different cases rhetorically; Milton's feat of constructing a double argument on the same words, each highly plausible and yet as different as light from darkness, is, so far as I know, unique in English literature. It is the supreme poetic statement of the dialectician in Milton, the poet who defended the freedom of the press on the ground that "this permission of free writing, were there no good else in it . . . is such an unripping, such an anatomy of the shyest and tenderest particular truths, as makes not only the whole nation in many points the wiser, but also presents and carries home to princes, and men most remote from vulgar concourse, such a full insight of every lurking evil."

The rejecting of the temptation of Rome forces Satan to relinquish one of his trump cards, which is the appeal to opportunity, the panic inspired by the ticking clock. The aspect of temptation which suggests the temporal also has a connection with Milton's own life and the collision of impulses to complete and postpone his masterpiece already referred to. This problem, in itself peculiar to Milton as a poet, was for him also a special case of the general principle that the Christian must learn to will to relax the will, to perform real acts in God's time and not pseudo-acts in his own. In the temptations of Adam and Samson the same theme recurs of an action not so much wrong in itself as wrong at that time, a hasty snatching of a chance before the real time has fulfilled itself. Christ is older than Milton was at twenty-three when he wrote his famous sonnet, and Satan is constantly urging him, from the first temptation on, to be his own providence, to release some of his own latent energies. The discipline of waiting is not only more difficult and inglorious, but constantly subject to the danger of passing insensibly into procrastination.

The subtlest thing that Satan says in the poem is his remark that

> each act is rightliest done,
> Not when it must, but when it may be best.

The demonic hero judges the present by an intuitive sense of the immediate future. He is distinguished from other men by his capacity to take thought for the morrow, to be in short a diviner. Thus Satan is a spokesman for that dark and forbidden future knowledge which we have spoken of as in the Classical epics gained from the gods below and not the gods above. We are not surprised to find that Satan's oracular powers in *Paradise Regained* include a knowledge of Christ's future "fate" gained by astrology. Christ's main scriptural ally in rejecting this temptation is Ecclesiastes, with its doctrine that there is a time for all things, but the sense of strain in waiting for God's time comes out in several places in the poem, from the reference to the lost tribes, already quoted, to the strain of the forty days' fast itself.

The temptation of Athens has, as its Antichrist core, the Stoic ideal, the "apathy" of the invulnerable individual who feels that the wise man in a bad world can only do the best he can for himself. This is the simple giving up of social action for individual improvement, which, as we saw in the previous chapter, was not the real meaning of the impact of the Restoration on Milton. In rejecting this temptation, Christ also rejects the contemplative life as an end: Christ's aim is to redeem the world, not to live a morally sinless life, which he might conceivably have done as a philosopher. In the temptation of Athens the clash of the two oracular traditions, the prophetic and the demonic, reaches its climax. Here again it is Greek philosophy in its context as part of Satan's kingdom that is being rejected. A Christian working outward from his faith might find the study of Plato and Aristotle profitable enough; but if he were to *exchange* the direct tradition of revelation for their doctrines, which is what Christ is being tempted to do, he would find in them only the fine flower of a great speculative tree, with its roots in the demonic metaphysics and theology described in the second book of *Paradise Lost*.

The third temptation begins with a night of storm, not in itself a temptation but an indispensable preliminary to one. Its object is to impress Christ with Satan's power as prince of an indifferent and mindless order of nature, to suggest that his Father has either forsaken him or is unable to reach him in a fallen world. It is, in short, another suggestion of despair or distrust, but with the specific aim of making Christ feel lonely and deserted, hence isolated, hence the self-contained ego which is the form of pride. It demonstrates the fact that in a world of death and mutability the light of nature is surrounded by the darkness of nature; but as Christ has already rejected all arguments based on the analogy of natural and revealed wisdom, this fact comes as no great surprise. The placing of Christ on the pinnacle of the temple follows and is, as Satan makes clear, a temptation of Jesus purely in his capacity as Son of God, an ordeal that no simple human nature would be able to survive. Here, for once, we can cautiously accept what Satan says, although of course his motive in saying it is to drop a suggestion of arrogance into Christ's mind.

The temptation of the pinnacle is equally a bodily and a mental assault. Christ has been weakened by forty days of fasting and by the night of storm. We saw that Satan won over

Eve by instilling thoughts into her mind while her consciousness was preoccupied with the wonder of a talking snake, so
that Eve, when she came to search her own mind, found Satan's
thoughts there and took them for her own. Christ is far more
astute, but still the sequence of blinding visions of earthly
glory may have left in his mind some faint trace of attachment,
some unconscious sense of exaltation. If so, he will feel dizzy
on the pinnacle. Mentally, then, Christ is being tested for
hybris, or pride of mind. He is in the position of a tragic hero,
on top of the wheel of fortune, subject to the fatal instant of
distraction that will bring him down.

Physically, Christ is being tested for exhaustion, for a slight
yielding to pressure that will make him stagger out of sheer
weariness. Satan quotes the Psalms to show that the Messiah
could fall, trusting in the support of angels; but Christ, though
led by the Spirit into the wilderness, is not being led by the
Spirit to fall off the pinnacle. That would be his own act,
and the Antichrist core of it would be a trust not in angels but
in his own fortune, or luck, and trusting to luck is the same
thing as trusting Satan. It would perhaps be a reasonable
definition of cowardice to say that a coward is a man whose
instinct it is, in a crisis, to do what his enemy wants him to do.
Christ's ordeal is one of fortitude as well as wisdom, and he has
proved himself no coward; but even brave men have had
traitors lurking within them, something that co-operated with
an outward attack. If there is the smallest trace either of pride
in Christ's mind or what we should now call the death-
impulse in his body—the impulse that would make any other
man accept the vinegar sponge on the cross—this final test
will reveal it. If not, Christ is ready to be God's sacrificial

victim, a martyr who, so far from being, like many martyrs, half in love with easeful death, dies as the implacable enemy of death.

Christ has thus far been tempted *quasi homo*, purely as man. For Milton, Christ, having resisted the whole of Satan's world, has done what man can do: he has come to the end of the negative and iconoclastic effort which is all that man as such can accomplish in aid of his own salvation. The only possible next step is for God to indicate acceptance of what has been done. Thus the fact that Christ successfully stands on the pinnacle is miraculous, but not a miracle drawn from his own divine nature, not an ace hidden up his sleeve, which is what Satan is looking for. It means that his human will has been taken over by the omnipotent divine will at the necessary point, and prefigures the commending of his spirit to the Father at the instant of his death on the cross.

Christ's answer, "Tempt not the Lord thy God," is the only remark Christ makes in the poem which employs ambiguity. Primarily, it means "Do not put the Father to unnecessary tests," the meaning of the passage in Deuteronomy which Jesus is quoting. But here the Son carries the name and nature of the Father, and the statement bears the secondary meaning "Do not continue the temptation of the Son of God." At this point, perhaps, Satan for the first time recognizes in Jesus his old antagonist of the war in heaven. Earlier in the poem he had spoken of Christ as an opaque cloud which might be a cooling or shading screen between himself and the wrath of the Father. This is, not surprisingly, the direct opposite of Christ's true nature

In whose conspicuous countenance, without cloud,
Made visible, the Almighty Father shines.

So far from screening the fire of the Father, the Son is focusing
it like a burning glass, the two natures of the Godhead united
as closely as Milton's Christology will permit. And just as this
last temptation was of Christ in his specific role as Son of God,
so with his victory Satan is defeated in his own headquarters,
the lower heaven or element of air which is the spatial limit
of his conquest at the fall. That is why Christ's victory is
immediately followed by a reference to the struggle of Hercules
and Antaeus, in which Hercules (a prototype of Christ also in
the Nativity Ode and elsewhere) overcame the monstrous son
of earth in the air.

There is a hidden irony in Satan's quotation from the
ninety-first Psalm. He quotes the eleventh and twelfth verses;
the thirteenth reads: "Thou shalt tread upon the lion and adder;
the young lion and the dragon shalt thou trample under feet."
In his fall Satan assumes the position of the dragon under
Christ's feet, the only place for him after his failure to gain
entrance to Christ's body or mind. At this point a new centre
of gravity is established in the world, as the gospel is finally
separated from the law. Judaism joins Classical wisdom as part
of the demonic illusion, as the centre of religion passes from
the temple Christ is standing on into the Christian temple, the
body of Christ above it. The destruction of the Garden of Eden
at the flood showed that God "attributes to place no sanctity,"
and the later destruction of the temple, prefigured at this point,
illustrates the same principle. Christ's casting the devils out of
heaven prefigured the cleansing of the temple, with which,

according to John, his ministry began. Here, with the end of the temptation, Christ has chased the devils out of the temple of his own body and mind and is ready to repeat the process for each human soul.

The temptation of the pinnacle corresponds to the point in *Samson Agonistes* at which Samson, after beating off Manoah, Delilah, and Harapha, refuses to go to the Philistine festival. He is right in refusing, but he has come to the end of his own will. At that point he appears to change his mind, but what has happened is that God has accepted his efforts and taken over his will. In *Samson Agonistes*, which is a tragedy, this point is the "peripety": Samson is now certain to die, though also certain of redemption. Jesus has also made it impossible for himself to avoid death, as his prototypes Elijah and perhaps Moses did; but *Paradise Regained* is not a tragedy, but an episode in the divine comedy, and we need another term for the crucial point of the action.

We have already met Milton's distinction between the literal and what he calls the metaphorical generation of the Son by the Father. The latter, we said, was epiphany, the manifesting of Christ in his divine capacity to others, and it is this epiphany and not literal generation that is taking place in the first chronological event of *Paradise Lost*. The same distinction recurs in the Incarnation. Two of the Gospels, Matthew and Luke, the two which give us the account of the temptation, are nativity Gospels: they begin with Christ's infancy or physical generation in the world. The other two, Mark and John, are epiphanic Gospels, and begin with the baptism, where Jesus is pointed out to man as the Son of God. (In the Western churches epiphany means particularly the showing of the infant

Christ to the Magi, but in the Eastern churches it means particularly the baptism.) Epiphany is the theological equivalent of what in literature is called "anagnorisis" or "recognition." The Father recognizes Jesus as the Son at the baptism: Satan recognizes him on the pinnacle in a different, yet closely related, sense. The action of *Paradise Regained* begins with the baptism, an epiphany which Satan sees but does not understand, and ends with an epiphany to Satan alone, the nature of which he can hardly fail to understand.

With the end of the temptation, Christ's work is essentially accomplished. The Passion itself, and more particularly the crucifixion, is also epiphanic, an exhibition to mankind of what Christ is and what he has done. The two poles of Christ's career on earth are the baptism and the crucifixion, both public events. And just as the crucifixion was followed by the resurrection, which was esoteric, shown only to Christ's followers, so the baptism is followed by a hidden event in which Christ disappears from the sight of mankind and then "Home to his mother's house private returned," the fate of the world having been changed in the meantime. *Paradise Regained* is the definitive statement in Milton of the dialectical separation of heaven from hell that reason based on revelation makes, and the individual nature of every act of freedom. To use terms which are not Milton's but express something of his attitude, the central myth of mankind is the myth of lost identity: the goal of all reason, courage and vision is the regaining of identity. The recovery of identity is not the feeling that I am myself and not another, but the realization that there is only one man, one mind, and one world, and that all walls of partition have been broken down forever.